HOMILIES IN A NEW KEY

HOMILIES IN A NEW KEY

Harvey D. Egan, SJ

Foreword by Joseph E. Weiss, SJ

WIPF & STOCK · Eugene, Oregon

HOMILIES IN A NEW KEY

Copyright © 2021 Harvey D. Egan, SJ. All rights reserved. Except for brief quotations in critical publications or reviews, no part of this book may be reproduced in any manner without prior written permission from the publisher. Write: Permissions, Wipf and Stock Publishers, 199 W. 8th Ave., Suite 3, Eugene, OR 97401.

Resource Publications
An Imprint of Wipf and Stock Publishers
199 W. 8th Ave., Suite 3
Eugene, OR 97401

www.wipfandstock.com

PAPERBACK ISBN: 978-1-6667-1917-8
HARDCOVER ISBN: 978-1-6667-1918-5
EBOOK ISBN: 978-1-6667-1919-2

MARCH 3, 2022

To my sister, Joyce, and in memory of my mother and father.

CONTENTS

Foreword | *xiii*

Acknowledgements | *xvii*

INTRODUCTION | 1

HOMILIES FOR SPECIAL FEAST DAYS

Homily 1
   ADVENT AND EXPECTATION | 7

Homily 2
   ADVENT: THE OLD AND THE NEW | 10

Homily 3
   THE VISITATION: TWO PREGNANT WOMEN | 12

Homily 4
   CHRISTMAS: CHRIST, LIGHT OF THE WORLD | 15

Homily 5
   EPIPHANY AS POLITICAL NITROGLYCERIN | 18

Homily 6
   NEW YEAR: HE WAS NAMED JESUS | 21

Homily 7
   THE PRESENTATION OF JESUS IN THE TEMPLE | 23

Homily 8
   FEAST OF THE HOLY FAMILY | 25

Homily 9
   CANA AND MARY | 28

Homily 10
   THE BAPTISM OF THE LORD | 31

Homily 11
    ASH WEDNESDAY AND GENUINE CHRISTIANITY | 33

Homily 12
    LENT: SATAN TESTS JESUS IN THE DESERT | 36

Homily 13
    RETHINKING GOOD FRIDAY AND THE CROSS | 39

Homily 14
    RETHINKING GOOD FRIDAY AS CHRIST'S DESCENT INTO HELL | 42

Homily 15
    RESURRECTION: IN NO OTHER NAME | 45

Homily 16
    JESUS' EASTER APPEARANCES | 48

Homily 17
    FEAST OF JESUS' BODY AND BLOOD | 51

Homily 18
    RETHINKING BLOOD SACRIFICE | 54

Homily 19
    EATING AND DRINKING CHRIST'S FLESH AND BLOOD | 56

Homily 20
    RETHINKING JESUS' ASCENSION | 59

Homily 21
    JESUS, THE BRIDEGROOM: RETHINKING HEAVEN | 62

Homily 22
    RETHINKING RESURRECTION AND HEAVEN AS THE NEW CREATION | 64

Homily 23
    FEAST OF CHRIST THE KING | 67

Homily 24
    PENTECOST SUNDAY | 70

Homily 25
    TRINITY SUNDAY | 73

HOMILIES CENTERED ON JESUS CHRIST

Homily 26
　　WHO DO YOU SAY THAT I AM? | 79

Homily 27
　　JESUS: CHRISTIANITY'S HEART | 81

Homily 28
　　JESUS' CENTRAL MESSAGE: THE KINGDOM | 83

Homily 29
　　JESUS THE JEW AND THE FEAST OF THE IMMACULATE HEART OF MARY | 85

Homily 30
　　JESUS' AUTHORITY | 88

Homily 31
　　HE WHO SEES ME SEES THE FATHER | 90

Homily 32
　　THE OFFENSIVE JESUS | 93

Homily 33
　　LOSING ONE'S LIFE FOR JESUS' SAKE | 96

Homily 34
　　JESUS AND POLITICS | 98

Homily 35
　　MUSTARD SEED AND THE KINGDOM OF GOD | 101

Homily 36
　　JESUS FORGIVES SINS | 103

Homily 37
　　JESUS CURES THE DEAF MUTE | 105

Homily 38
　　JESUS CALMS THE VIOLENT SEAS | 108

Homily 39
　　JESUS FEEDS THE MULTITUDES | 111

Homily 40
　　THE PROPHET ELISHA AND JESUS FEED THE MULTITUDES | 114

Homily 41
    JESUS THE EUNUCH, BARREN WOMEN, AND THE KINGDOM | 117

Homily 42
    JESUS AND WOMEN I | 119

Homily 43
    JESUS AND WOMEN II | 122

Homily 44
    NO ONE KNOWS THE SON EXCEPT THE FATHER | 125

Homily 45
    HE'S OUT OF HIS MIND | 128

HOMILIES ON SIGNIFICANT CHRISTIAN TRUTHS

Homily 46
    THE POWER OF FAITH | 133

Homily 47
    SUFFERING FOR THE KINGDOM OF GOD | 135

Homily 48
    PRAY UNCEASINGLY | 137

Homily 49
    BE RICH IN WHAT MATTERS TO GOD | 140

Homily 50
    THE LORD'S PRAYER AND AGING | 143

Homily 51
    PARABLE OF THE WEDDING FEAST | 146

Homily 52
    A WORTHY WIFE | 149

Homily 53
    CHILDREN AS GIFT AND CELIBACY | 153

Homily 54:
    CHILDREN: THE GREATEST IN GOD'S KINGDOM | 155

Homily 55
    JULY FOURTH—INDEPENDENCE DAY | 157

Homily 56
    REJOICING IN THE ANNIVERSARY OF MY JESUIT VOCATION | 160

Homily 57
    RETHINKING PURGATORY | 163

Homily 58
    RETHINKING HELL | 166

Homily 59
    JAIRUS'S DAUGHTER: CHRISTIAN PESSIMISM AND OPTIMISM | 169

HOMILIES FOR THE FEAST OF SAINTS

Homily 60
    THE CALL OF THE APOSTLE MATTHEW | 175

Homily 61
    PETER THE PARADOX | 177

Homily 62
    PETER WALKS ON THE WATER | 179

Homily 63
    MARY MAGDALENE AT THE TOMB AND NEW CREATION | 182

Homily 64
    FEAST OF SAINTS PAUL AND PETER | 184

Homily 65
    PAUL: THE ECSTATIC MYSTIC | 186

Homily 66
    ST. FRANCIS OF ASSISI'S STIGMATA AND THE STIGMATA OF DAILY LIFE | 188

Homily 67
    FRANCIS OF ASSISI AND IGNATIUS LOYOLA | 190

Homily 68
    THE FEAST OF IGNATIUS OF LOYOLA | 193

Homily 69
    FEAST OF TERESA OF AVILA | 196

Homily 70
    FEAST OF THE HOLY ANGELS | 198

Homily 71
    THE FEAST OF MARTYRS AND JESUS' PRESENCE AND ABSENCE | 201

Homily 72
    MOTHER TERESA: WRESTLING WITH GOD | 203

HOMILIES FOR FAMILY OCCASIONS

Homily 73
    A HOMILY FOR BAPTISM | 207

Homily 74
    A MARRIAGE HOMILY | 209

Homily 75
    A FUNERAL HOMILY | 213

Homily 76
    EULOGY FOR A BEST FRIEND | 216

FOREWORD

Joseph E Weiss, SJ

IN THE MID-TWENTIETH CENTURY, prior to the Second Vatican Council, the place of the Scriptures was minimal in the celebration of the Mass and Sunday preaching was optional. When a sermon was given, it came after the announcements, which directly followed the reading of the Gospel. To say there was a disconnect between the Gospel and the sermon would be an understatement. Rooted neither in the Scriptures nor the liturgy, the sermon, when given, offered catechetical and moral guidance.

The first action of the Council was a reform of Roman Catholic liturgy and with it a call for the restoration of the biblical, liturgical homily. At its final session in the autumn of 1965 the Council asserted that "the liturgical homily must hold the foremost place" within "the ministry of the word."[1] The reform of the liturgy and the reordering of the Mass into the Liturgy of the Word and the Liturgy of the Eucharist has restored the primacy of the presences of Christ in both the celebrations of Word and Sacrament. The revised Lectionary with its three-year cycle of Sunday readings and the two-year cycle of weekday readings provides a richer and deeper encounter for the faith community and the individual Christian with the living Word of God.

---

1. Second Vatican Council, *Dogmatic Constitution on Divine Revelation* (*Dei Verbum*), 24. Accessed at http://www.vatican.va/archive/hist_councils/ii_vatican-council/documents/vatii_const-19651118_dei-verbum_en.html.

FOREWORD

Today the primacy of God's Word in the liturgy requires preaching that brings into dialogue the encounter between God and the Church. The homily therefore is liturgical preaching rooted in the Scriptures, for a particular community of faith, addressing their lived experience of discipleship, in their daily life, in their culture, and in the world. Just as Jesus opened the Scriptures for the disciples on the road to Emmaus, so the homily, when true to its nature, opens for a particular faith community God's Word living and active among them.

The homily, like the Scriptures, is intended to be heard. It is intended to elicit a response of faith, first through the celebration of the liturgy of the Eucharist and second, by being sent to live our faith in daily life. Or in the words of Pope Francis being "missionary disciples." It is the ministry of the homilist to mediate the living encounter of the faith community with God's Word. To do so, the preacher must "believe what you read, teach what you believe, and practice what you teach."[2] So that the Word proclaimed may challenge and console, comfort and correct, enlighten and increase the faith, hope and love of the homilist and hearers.

While by its very nature the homily is an event that addresses a living community of faith in the here and now, still reading homilies and sermons spoken in the distant and recent past can continue to address the present and evoke the reader's own fresh response. Homilies that speak to everyday personal, ecclesial, and societal issues can enrich and inspire those who read them. Such is this collection: *Homilies in a New Key* by Harvey D. Egan, SJ.

"The primary duty of priests is the proclamation of the Gospel of God to all,"[3] states the Second Vatican Council. During his fifty-two years of priestly ministry, Fr. Egan has faithfully proclaimed the Gospel of God to all: students, scholars, contemplatives, parishioners, yes, even Jesuits! A former doctoral student of Karl Rahner, an expert in Christian mysticism and New Testament scholarship, Fr. Egan brings years of careful study, vast knowledge, and humanity to his preaching. Prepared for the faith community that gathers to celebrate the Eucharist on Sundays and weekdays in St. Mary's Chapel on the campus of Boston College, this collection of homilies is arranged not according to the Church Year but by topic for personal

---

2. *Rites of Ordination of a Bishop, Priest, and Deacon* (second typical edition), (Washington DC.: United States Conference of Catholic Bishops, 2003), 143.

3. Second Vatican Council, Decree on the Ministry and Life of Priests, (*Presbyterorum Ordinis*), 4. Accessed at http://www.vatican.va/archive/hist_councils/ii_vatican-council/documents/vatii_decree_19651207_presbyterorum-ordinin_en.html.

FOREWORD

prayer and meditation: liturgical feasts, Jesus Christ, miscellaneous topics, the feasts of the saints, and special family occasions.

Ten years after the close of Vatican II, St. Pope Paul VI wrote in Evangelii Nuntiandi: "The split between the Gospel and culture is without a doubt the drama of our times, just as it was in other times. Therefore every effort must be made to ensure a full evangelization of culture, or more correctly cultures. They have to be regenerated by an encounter with the Gospel.[4] *Homilies in a New Key* provides preachers and listeners, readers both, material for reflection and a new encounter with the Gospel.

Joseph E. Weiss, SJ, PhD
Professor of the Practice of Liturgy and Homiletics
School of Theology and Ministry
Boston College

---

4. Paul VI, apostolic exhortation on Evangelization in the Modern World (*Evangelii Nuntiandi*) 20. Accessed at https://www.vatican.va/content/paul-vi/en/apost_exhortations/documents/hf_p-vi_exh_19751208_evangelii-nuntiandi.html

ACKNOWLEDGEMENTS

I THANK THOSE WHO over the years have either heard or read these homilies. But I am especially grateful to those urging me to make them available for a wider audience: my almost lifelong friend, Lyla Baldwin; Sister Mary Augustine, lsp; and Norman Gordon. I would have never had them published without their prevailing upon me.

INTRODUCTION

These homilies being presented to you here are the product, in part, of over sixty years of Jesuit spirituality, philosophical-theological study, graduate and undergraduate university teaching, scholarly research and publishing, and pastoral experience as well. They reflect years of prayerfully contemplating and thinking deeply about the great Christian heritage in the context of the Second Vatican Council, the recent biblical, historical, and theological scholarship, and contemporary issues arising in American culture. More specifically, behind these homilies, there stand, unobtrusively, the philosophical-theological thinking of Karl Rahner and Bernard Lonergan, the historical work of Bernard McGinn on the Christian mystical tradition, and the outstanding biblical scholarship of N. T. Wright. And yet my homilies attempt to remain faithful to the Mass readings and to the catechism of the hearts of those worshipping and prayerfully drinking in God's word addressed to them.

As a Jesuit who takes seriously Ignatius of Loyola's emphasis on "safe doctrine" (by which I do not mean a naive fundamentalism) my homilies *rethink*—creatively but in an orthodox way—significant aspects of Christianity. Pope Francis claims that homilies are a torture both for those preparing and for those hearing them. That may be true, but I view crafting and delivering a good homily a challenge to enrich spiritually not only the congregation but also the homilist. One friend wisely compared good homilies to good home-cooking. One might not be able to remember much over the years about what was actually cooked, but one was indeed nourished. May you find these homilies spiritually nourishing.

I have never shared the views of those who regard homilies as treatises on scriptural interpretation, or as highly technical theology, or as a platform for expressing the homilist's political views—or worse, as an occasion to speak merely off the top of one's head. The good and bad homilies of others, the dependence on excellent contemporary biblical commentaries, scholarly theological work, classroom and seminar experience, years of pastoral involvement, and the weekly news almost always catalyzed and gave me a few ideas and a starting point for my own homily. The now deceased Jesuit, former classmate, and first-rate scripture scholar Daniel Harrington, who preached almost every Sunday and feast days at a Boston-area church, delighted in telling the story of a parishioner who came up to him after Mass and said, "Father, I used to find your homilies quite boring—until I began to listen to them." The highly-respected Episcopalian priest, scholar, author, and homilist Rutledge Fleming maintained that any homily less than an hour was not a true homily and also complained that some people often did not listen to her. Her views on these matters are hardly consonant with contemporary western life and with my own homiletic style.

After almost fifty years of teaching and giving homilies, however, I take comfort in the fact that even Jesus' disciples fell asleep in his presence. When St. Anthony of Padua preached to people—with hardened hearts who would not listen to him—he went to the nearby sea and preached to the fish. Gathering in huge schools to listen to his homilies, the fish—with their heads out of the water, bowed their heads, and with these and other signs of reverence—they glorified God as much as was in their power. Upon seeing this, the townspeople changed their attitude and began to profit from his homilies. Over the course of many years, I have befriended killer whales, porpoises, pit bulls, an orangutan, and even a once local, domesticated Alaskan wolf. So, I already had and have a ready and willing audience.

Students at both Santa Clara University and Boston College told me that they appreciated my homilies for being so *existential*—and this was not said out of politeness. Santa Clara Carmelite nuns deemed them *exceptional*. When I served as a chaplain at Mercy Hospital in San Diego, some nuns took notes when I presented homilies. Jesuits are not inclined to praise their fellow Jesuits, but many have informed me of just how helpful my homilies were. It astonished me how often people just before receiving Communion from my hands would tell me how much they like the homily and how *deep* it was. Some time ago I told an atheist Jewish friend that I was working on my Sunday homily. He asked to read it. Then he asked for the later ones, which he distributed to his friends. He pressed me to get them published. I am deeply aware, however, that the word *spoken* and *heard* is often more powerful that the one that is written and read.

INTRODUCTION

One reader of this manuscript alerted me to some repetition in the homilies. As a professor for about forty years, I appreciate the dictum: "Repetition is the mother of learning." Popular misunderstandings about particular truths of the faith demand that some key points be repeated. Giving the same homily to different congregations occasions repetition and variation. To be sure, I have some favorite stories and illustrations for whose repetition I make no apologies. Lastly, unlike most books, a collection of homilies should not be read in their given order but with selection for specific occasion.

I have the audacity and the confidence, therefore, to present these homilies that focus on special liturgical feasts, on Jesus Christ, on spiritual topics, on the feasts of celebrated saints, and on special family occasions. They might serve as guides for other homilists, as material for critical consideration by homiletics professors, and as spiritual reading for anyone interested in the content. But I sincerely pray that these homilies will help you to know Christ better, stir you to love him more deeply, and embolden you to follow him more closely.

HOMILIES FOR SPECIAL FEAST DAYS

Homily 1

ADVENT AND EXPECTATION

"Therefore, stay awake. Be prepared!"

THE CHURCH'S ADVENT SEASON reminds us that everyone, not only a Christian, is a person of expectation, anticipation, longing, yearning, waiting. "Therefore, stay awake!" How we dislike waiting! Dorothy Day maintained that the poor are forced to wait more than anyone else. In Samuel Beckett's absurdist play, *Waiting for Godot*, two characters, Vladimir and Estragon (good names for a dog?), wait endlessly and in vain for the arrival of someone named Godot. The salient way this play captures the haunting expectation, advent, rooted in every human heart is stunning.

The teenager in the novel, *The Heart is a Lonely Hunter*, also highlights the heart's immense longing. She says to her parents: "I feel that something really big is going to happen to me." Her mother cruelly retorts: "I felt the same way when I was your age. You'll get over it." The mother is wrong; we never get over it.

We all yearn for the one purchase (look at the Black Friday crowds), the one event (getting into our choice university, promotion, manuscript accepted for publication), the one person (is he or she the one to be my spouse?) that will totally fulfill us. If you had one wish, what would you wish for? Be very careful because when you get what you want, will you want what you get?

This morning's first reading and responsorial psalm both focus on the Jerusalem Temple. If you were to combine in one place the functions of St. Peter's basilica in Rome, Wall Street, the White House, the Federal Reserve, and the Pentagon, then you would have an idea of how central the Jerusalem Temple was to Jewish life and expectations. The desire in the prophet Isaiah's heart in this morning's reading and Jewish expectations in the Jesus' time—Jewish Advent—coincide: God *will* be faithful to his covenant promises, finally and permanently dwell in the fully restored Jerusalem Temple, forgive the Jews their sins, free them from pagan rule them by kicking out the Roman occupiers, and over-throwing the pseudo-king Herod. Then the Jews will be what God through Moses had promised them: to be the light of the nations that brings salvation and peace to the whole world. Jesus also stresses this: "Salvation is from the Jews." And note how *this* worldly the Jews and Jesus understood the kingdom of God.

God the Father, however, sent his Son, Jesus Christ, to be the fulfillment and transformation of all Jewish yearning: Jesus, the true light of the world; Jesus, the enfleshed, personal kingdom. In him one finds total human fulfillment. It had been revealed to Simeon—who yearned for the consolation of Israel—that he would not die before he had seen the Lord's anointed, the Christ. And he does, when Jesus is presented in the Temple.

Yet notice how even John the Baptist, the highpoint of Jewish spirituality, gets his Advent longings wrong and asks of Jesus-Messiah: "Are you the one who is to come or should we look for another?" The Emmaus disciples also get it wrong: "We had hoped that he was the one to redeem Israel." The apostles ask Jesus after the resurrection, "Lord, will you at this time restore the kingdom to Israel?" On the other hand, the apostle Paul imprisoned in Rome got it right. Even though the Romans still ruled, Herod was still king, Paul never wavered in his belief that Jesus and Jesus alone is the messiah, the Lord, and the seed of the kingdom of God. Do we get it right?

I was asked point blank recently if, given my age and health, I were waiting for, expecting, death. In this Advent season, I wait for, expect the risen Christ, and pray the final words of the Scriptures, "Come Lord Jesus, come." The great Jesuit scientist-mystic, Teilhard de Chardin, complained that Christians no longer expect anything. Moreover, I look forward to, await, the new heavens and the new earth, as depicted in the Book of Revelation—*not* heaven the way it is usually understood as out or up there—but here, transformed. The *Boston Globe* writer, Alex Beam, started a ruckus a while back when he claimed that dogs will be in heaven. My view: of course! I've had many family dogs, kissed a killer whale, nuzzled an Alaskan wolf, danced with an orangutan, and surfed with porpoises. I fully expect to see them again—transformed, resurrected.

ADVENT AND EXPECTATION

The Advent season should remind us that the risen Jesus is the seed of the new heavens and the new earth, which will consist not only of us as resurrected and transformed but also of the earth, oceans, lakes, streams, valleys, mountains, plants, trees, animals, stars, sun—in short, everything created now—*resurrected and transformed*. What God has created, he loves and will bring to total fulfillment. I await not only seeing my mother and again, but also our family dogs and our perky canary Mario. I know, too, that my orangutan friend is looking forward to dancing with me again. "Come Lord Jesus come."

Homily 2

ADVENT: THE OLD AND THE NEW

"The least in the kingdom of heaven is greater than John the Baptist."

WHEN I WROTE MY dissertation in Germany in the early nineteen-seventies, I used a manual typewriter and carbon paper. The younger Jesuits laugh when I tell them this fact. However, the old ways did work—with much work. Now, whenever I write, I have my computer, two word-processing programs, a scanner, and an excellent speech recognition program. The old and the new: John the Baptist and Jesus.

This morning's gospel underscores Jesus' knowledge of Malachi's prediction, "See, I will send the prophet Elijah to you before that great and dreadful day of the Lord comes." He also assigns the role of prophet who ushers in the age to come to John the Baptist—whom he claimed was the greatest of those born from women. Still, Jesus-Messiah contends that the least in God's kingdom is greater than John. I have long been fascinated that John the Baptist, the high point of Jewish spirituality, failed to understand Jesus as Israel's true messiah and asked, "Are you he who is to come or should we look for another?" Jesus says essentially that the old days and ways of trying to bring in God's kingdom, Israel fulfilled and this earth renewed and healed—as predicted by Isaiah in the first reading—are over. The days of the old typewriter are over. Jesus inaugurates the true kingdom of God in his person and in his own way through his exorcisms, parables, healings, miracles, and raising people from the dead. Jesus-Messiah is the true king of the universe and no one else.

ADVENT: THE OLD AND THE NEW

Pope Francis's recent encyclical on the environment, *Laudato si' (Praise Be to You)*, brings out the full meaning of the kingdom and Jesus-Messiah as king. He wrote that the ultimate destiny of the entire universe is in the fullness of God, which has already been attained by the risen Christ. Did not the apostle Paul write that in Jesus all things have been created, in him all things hold together—and that because of Jesus, God shall be all and in all? Does not the Book of Revelation teach that the Messiah-King-Lamb who sits on the throne makes all things new and that every creature in the new heaven and on the new earth and under the earth and in the sea, and all that is in them, shall praise and worship the slain lamb.

I was speaking a while back with a sickly old man and he mentioned that his golden retriever dog, "Chance," had died. When I told him that he would see Chance again, he began to cry. I maintain that Jesus, the Messiah-King, is not only the king of humans and angels, but also of animals, insects, vegetation, rivers, oceans, the sun, the moon—the king also of the entire future new earth and the new heaven. In any of my homilies that refer in any way to new creation, I emphasize that I've kissed a killer whale, danced with an orangutan, surfed with dolphins, nuzzled an Alaskan wolf, and always had family dogs. I fully expect to see them again. As the prophet Isaiah concludes in this morning first reading: "The hand of the Lord has done this, the Holy One of Israel has created it."

Homily 3

THE VISITATION: TWO PREGNANT WOMEN

"Blessed is the fruit of your womb."

This morning's gospel focuses on the six-months pregnant Elizabeth and her also pregnant cousin, the blessed Virgin Mary. When they meet, Elizabeth—who suffered mentally for many years because of her infertility—cries out that the infant in her womb leaped for joy. Then she calls Mary, "the mother of *my Lord*." Very early, the church used this text to designate Mary as "God-bearer"—Lord, being the Greek Old Testament name for God.

As I prayed over this text, I thought of my mother and a close family friend, in adjacent maternity-ward beds, who gave birth to baby girls the same day. My sister and the other daughter Marsha are still close friends. "Blessed is the fruit of your womb." The mighty warrior Jephthah the Gileadite promised God that he would sacrifice the first Israelite he met on his way home, if he were victorious against the Ammonites. Unfortunately that person turned out to be his own daughter. She told him to fulfill his vow but also to allow her to spend two months in the mountains to mourn her virginity. When some students snicker when I tell this story, I remind them that for a Jewish woman no worst shame existed than being childless. In some ways, it was a living death— an affliction still true in some parts of the contemporary world. Elizabeth of this morning's gospel had so suffered. Contrast this with Jesus' *woeful* beatitude: Blessed are the barren, the

THE VISITATION: TWO PREGNANT WOMEN

wombs that never gave birth—a prophecy of the trials that would befall those when the Roman occupiers would destroy Jerusalem and its Temple.

I know a marvelous woman here at Boston College who was told by doctors that she would never have children. The sheer joy on her face when she related to me that one morning—after seven years of marriage—she exclaimed: "I'm pregnant." She now has two lovely children. "Blessed is the fruit of your womb." Years ago a former graduate student came to the Jesuit residence at Boston College to see me. It was evident that she was pleasingly pregnant. She told me that doctors advised her to abort because the baby would either be born dead or live only a short time. With an incredible peace that only faith in the crucified and risen Lord can give, however, she and her husband had firmly decided to have the baby. A few months later she met with me again. The baby had been born, baptized, and named *Elizabeth*—this morning's gospel. Baby Elizabeth died a few weeks later, a funeral was held, and Elizabeth was buried. "Blessed is the fruit of your womb." Recently I was speaking with an old friend who had an abortion in her youth and still has not gotten over it. It reminded me that although the Japanese do not stigmatize abortion either religiously or culturally, many Japanese woman who abort have a statue made of the dead child and place it in a temple. "Blessed is the fruit of your womb." Contrast this with a woman I knew who used to date my best friend. She told me privately that she would never marry him because he wanted children and if she ever became pregnant, she would commit suicide.

Not infrequently when I read the newspapers or watch TV news, I understand why the Bible proclaims its most pessimistic words: "God repented that he had made man." Still, when I ponder the words, "blessed is the fruit of your womb," Christianity's profoundest and most optimistic mystery spring to mind: "The Word became flesh, human, and dwelt among us." The Judeo-Christian tradition reverences human beings not only because God deemed everything he had made as "good" but also because we are created in God's image and likeness.

True Christianity despises nothing: marriage, conjugal relations, conception, pregnancy, labor pains, births, breast feeding, infants, toddlers, bodily functions, seven-hundred gallons of water changed into wine at Cana, feasts, food—plenty of bread and fish multiplied. I do object to Jesus' limited menu.

Do we not rejoice when we hear, see, and touch a loved one. The glory of being a *body* person. The word became flesh and Jesus' disciples had the privilege to experience this. As the First Epistle of John proclaims: "We declare to you what we have *heard*, what we have *seen* with our eyes, what we have *looked at* and *touched* with our hands, concerning the word of life," the crucified, risen, and ascended Lord. "Blessed is the fruit of your womb."

Homily 4

CHRISTMAS: CHRIST, LIGHT OF THE WORLD

"The people who sit in darkness have seen a great light!"

IF YOU HAVE BEEN enveloped by pitch blackness in the wilderness or even a room looking for a light switch, then you can appreciate the value of light. The first reading from one of the Christmas Masses focuses on the prophet Isaiah's text concerning the *light of the world*, probably the most important messianic text in the Jewish scriptures. Christians have long confessed Jesus-Messiah to be *the light of the world.*

The very first page of the Scriptures states: "In the beginning darkness was over the surface of the deep, and God said, 'Let there be light,' and there was *light*. And God saw that the light was *good*." The first letter of John proclaims: "God *is* light; in him there is no darkness at all." In one of the Hobbit movies, *Smaug*, the evil dragon brags: "There is no light that can defeat the darkness." However, the very beginning of John's Gospel contradicts this in which he announces: "The light shines in the darkness, and the darkness has *not* overcome it."

I know a person who had cataract surgery in both eyes and found the light and color so vivid when he entered his fitness club that he ran out to put on sunglasses. The goodness and blessing of light—the right light. Exclusive and even not so exclusive department stores, jewelry stores, advertisers, car shows, restaurants, and so on, know the importance of the right light. Studies have shown that a certain light on even repulsive foods makes them look appetizing and the wrong light even on normally delicious foods makes them look unappetizing.

The first chapter of John's Gospel proclaims that God's creative *light and life have become flesh*: "In the beginning was the Word and through him all things were made. In him was life, and that life was the light of all humankind." If God *is* light, the light through which everything is created and has light, it is no wonder that some cultures worshipped the sun—and have people who stay up all night to make certain the sun comes up in the morning. The Scriptures clearly view darkness as linked with chaos and even evil. The devil is called the "prince of darkness," a name one superior frequently called me because of my fondness for dimming the lights in the dining room. Some of my wise-cracking students used to call me Darth Vader, Dark Father. Nevertheless, one demon is named Lucifer, light-bearing, morning star. Paul writes that "Satan himself masquerades as an angel of light." I think of Vegas, bars, discos, places for recreational drug use, pole dancing habitats, rock concerts, Miley Cyrus's twerking—the way the *false* lights of the world are used to seduce.

When going over today's readings, two experiences immediately came to mind. The first: I was quite struck recently by how attractive a young woman looked exercising. But when she stepped out of the light dominating the area, she looked most ordinary. So, even I could look good in a certain light. The importance of the right light. Second: the apostle Paul's experience on the Damascus road of the light of the risen Christ. In one of the most beautiful texts ever written, Paul states: "For God, who said, 'let light shine out of darkness,' has shone in our hearts to give the *light* of the knowledge of the glory of God in the face of Jesus Christ." This is also the glory that left the Jerusalem Temple when the Babylonians sacked Jerusalem and destroyed the Temple—which the prophets foretold would return to a newly built Temple, who is Jesus-Messiah, the new Temple, the light of the world. So bright was the light from Moses' face when he came down the mountain that the Israelites feared him. Jesus' disciples cried out at his transfiguration, "it is good for us to be here."

Malcolm Muggeridge was converted in part by the light emanating from Mother Teresa's face. The early Jesuits were awed by the light flowing from the face of St. Ignatius. When I perform a wedding, I am always struck by the light in a bride's face. Ever notice how a face lights up when a loved one enters the room. What of the old song, "you light up my life?" (Want me to sing it for you?)

CHRISTMAS: CHRIST, LIGHT OF THE WORLD

From that moment on the Damascus road, Paul saw everything in the light from the risen Christ. This light was so subversive that the apostle could write to Philemon about Onesimus, the runaway slave: "Perhaps the reason Onesimus was separated from you for a little while was that you might have him back forever—*no longer as a slave, but better than a slave, as a dear brother. So if you consider me a partner, welcome him as you would welcome me.*" How radical—in a culture where slavery was woven into the very fabric of society. In the light of Christ, a slave is a brother, even Paul's double. Paul also insisted that in Christ there is neither Jew nor Gentile, neither slave nor free, nor is there male and female, for you are all one in Jesus-Messiah.

How utterly revolutionary! In the light of Christ, we are all equal, all brothers and sisters in the Lord. Jesus said: "*you* are the light of the world." We should therefore see others— regardless of race, color, or creed—in this light. If it takes faith to see the crucified and risen Christ in the eucharistic bread and wine, we should apply that faith to everyone we meet. One mystic wrote of seeing everyone and everything, even evil, in the light from Christ's glorious wounds.

Finally, when Jesus ascended into heaven, he said to his disciples: "I'll leave the light on for you." Christmas: the birthday of the Light of the world.

Homily 5

EPIPHANY AS POLITICAL NITROGLYCERIN

"We, the Magi, saw his star when it rose and have come to worship him."

WHEN I WAS A boy, my father's explanation of the different constellations in the night sky always brought me great joy. And how we both loved the brilliant planet Venus but found the planet Mars eerie. And years later, it delighted me no end to show not only my nieces and nephew but also later my grandnieces and grandnephew the constellations in the night sky. I had the great blessing to be awed by the night sky in an Australian desert and by the extraordinary Aurora Borealis both in the skies of Michigan's upper peninsula and in the Alaskan wilderness. Much publicity was given to the no-show comet Kohoutek in 1973 and then the 1997 comet Hale-Bopp that led the Heaven's Gate cult to commit mass suicide in the hope that they would reach a higher level of existence in the extraterrestrial space ship that was allegedly following the comet.

The night sky also fascinated the people of the ancient world who carefully observed the stars and the planets, even giving each one a very particular meaning. They believed that everything—earth and the heavens—was interconnected. Thus, when something important was about to happen on earth, they expected to see it reflected in the heavens.

The gospel readings of the past several weeks contain an angelic epiphany, revelation: to Mary, that she is to bear God's very own son; to Joseph, that his wife to be is pregnant with no less than Emmanuel, God-with-us;

EPIPHANY AS POLITICAL NITROGLYCERIN

to the shepherds, that the savior-messiah is to be found in a manger; to Simeon, that he now sees the consolation of Israel; to Anna, who knows that the child Jesus is Israel's redeemer.

Despite a cartoonist's claim this week, the bright light that fascinated the pagan astrologers, the Magi, was not a surface to air missile fired from a fighter bomber. It was likely the *conjunction* of the planets Jupiter, Mars, and Saturn. The Jews considered Jupiter to be the royal or kingly planet and Saturn was sometimes thought to represent the Jews. It was obvious: a new king of the Jews was about to be born. So, the pagan astrology of the three wise men—made precise by the Jewish scriptures—(you would think the rich Magi would have had a GPS) pointed to Bethlehem of Judea where they, gentiles, and pagans, would find and worship the true king—not only of the Jews but also of the world. Jesus is about to be revealed to the larger non-Jewish world. The gifts of gold, frankincense, and myrrh were what people in the ancient world thought appropriate for kings, and even gods. Not mentioned in the gospel, however, is the fourth Magi who brought a fruit cake—and the three wise women who brought casseroles, pampers, and baby formula.

Shortly before he died, the atheist Christopher Hitchens said that babies are cute, threaten no one, so Christmas really has no meaning. But the story of the Magi visiting Jesus is political nitroglycerine. This gospel makes clear that Jesus is the true king of the Jews, Herod is an imposter, and that even the claims of divinity by the great Caesar Augustus are bogus. Thus, the shadow of the cross falls across Jesus' head right from the start. He's born with a price on his head. Plots are hatched; an angel must warn Joseph who whisks Mary and the baby away just in time from Bethlehem.

Herod the Great, who did not hesitate to kill members of his own family (including his own beloved wife) because he suspected them of scheming against him, who gave orders when dying that the leading citizens of Jericho should be slaughtered so that there would be people weeping at his funeral—this Herod thought nothing of killing all the babies of an entire village in case one of them should be regarded as a royal pretender—just as Pharaoh had ordered the killing of all male babies born to the enslaved Jews in Egypt, and ISIS, Al Qaeda, Boko Haram, and others in our day have no qualms about killing even babies. I also underscore the massive slaughter of the unborn throughout the world.

This story also points ahead to the climax of the gospel where Jesus will finally come face-to-face with Caesar's subordinate, Pilate, the representative of the world's greatest emperor. Pilate will have rather different gifts to give Jesus, though he, too, is warned by his wife's dream not to do anything to him. Yet Pilate gets one thing right: he had a sign put on the cross that read: "Jesus of Nazareth, the king of the Jews."

His soldiers are the first gentiles since the Magi to call Jesus the king of the Jews, mockingly of course, for they crown him with thorns and give him a cross as his throne. At that moment, instead of a bright star, the sun, darkness falls upon the earth—and then we hear a pagan centurion utter an incredible truth: "This man truly was the Son of God!" And within a generation, Jesus' followers would be persecuted by the Roman empire and by later empires, large and small, as we find with Isis and other brutes in our own day. We had a Congolese Jesuit here at Boston College getting his doctorate who fully expects one day to be killed by his government.

What nonsense that Christianity is a private matter with nothing to do with politics. Jesus was a first-century Palestinian Jew whose central message focused on the kingdom of God—not universal love—as one often hears. And, the kingdom of God is very much of this world, with strong political overtones. Jesus did not say "my kingdom is not of this world," but my kingdom is not *from* this world. How can "thy kingdom come," a kingdom where justice and love must reign, have nothing to do with this world and with politics? So, with the Magi, let us this morning resolve to know, love, and serve the world's true light and king, and resolve to change our lives, as Isaiah wrote, walk by his light, and like the Magi, go back by a different route.

Homily 6

NEW YEAR: HE WAS NAMED JESUS

"He was named Jesus!"

IN JAMES MICHENER'S NOVEL, *Hawaii*, a married, childless, Chinese man migrates to Hawaii, finds suitable employment, and starts a new life with a common law wife—a clever, hard-working, and delightful woman. Their first child, a son, is born and named Wo-Chu. According to Chinese custom, the common law wife is now called Wo-Chu's *auntie*, while the *legal* but not biological mother in China is called Wo-Chu's *mommy*. As the years go by, auntie's family grows and become exceedingly wealthy. For financial reasons, the family prevails upon the one-hundred- year old, but still very shrew, "auntie" to become an American citizen.

After much cajoling, she agrees. But when the American official asks for her real name, the family demands that she remain silent. Auntie retorts: "You wanted me to become an American citizen. Americans use their real name. My given name is 'Guan-Yin Jiang.'" The family gasps. The power and dignity of a name, identity—regained even in old age.

It is astonishing how important a *name* is in the Bible. A google search yields hundreds of texts. For example, God grants Adam and Eve the power to *name* the animals, a way of indicating dominance. When younger, I jogged the Chestnut Hill area and always learned the names of the local dogs, which, when shouted if they chased me, usually stopped them cold. "Brutus, you stop that!" When Moses asked God for his name, perhaps to have some control over him, God replied: "I am who I am." In other words, mind your business; I cannot be controlled; I am above every name. Jews have such respect for God's name, Yahweh, that it is pronounced only once a year and written as four dots. Even God is written as G-D.

The Our Father prayer contains the phrase: "hallowed be thy name." When conquering armies ridiculed the Jews by blaspheming God's name, God said through the prophet Ezekiel, "I will show the holiness of my great *name*, which has been profaned among the nations. Then the nations will know that I am the Lord." My sister was very careful in naming her children because she knew first-hand how cruel children can be with names. Unfortunately, her first daughter, Donna, became known as "Donut." My brother-in-law was so eager to be a grandfather that he often pestered his son and daughter-in-law to have children. When a grandson finally arrived and began to speak, my brother-in-law was devastated that his grandson called him "popop." I told him that he was blessed to be given a unique grand name. Years ago, one older Jesuit who did not especially warm up to me—hard to believe—called me "Herv," with an edge. His name was Leo so I called him "Ao," maybe with an edge.

As a member of the society of *Jesus*, I have great love for the name "Jesus," which means "God saves." St Paul writes: "God has bestowed on him the *name* that is above every name, so that at the *name* of Jesus every knee should bow, in heaven and on earth and under the earth." So, I would sometimes bend my knee when someone cursed, "Jesus Christ," or even *jeez*. Jesus claimed that whatever we ask for in his *name* will be given—that he would send the Spirit in his *name*. The disciples and the early Christians preached "in the name of Jesus," and were astonished at the power of his name to heal and to drive out demons. They often baptized, forgave sins, and anointed the sick *in the name of Jesus*. The apostle Paul proclaimed that everyone who calls upon the name of the Lord will be save.

Despite my respect for some of the other religions of the world, I take seriously what the apostle Peter professed when he was on trial: "Salvation is found in *no other name* under heaven." We heard on the feast of the Holy Family the sentence: "Whatever you do, do it all in the *name* of the Lord Jesus." At the start of a confession, I often say, "May Jesus be in your hearts and on your lips." Some Christian mystics urged praying by simply repeating Jesus' name and breathing in a way to bring his name into one's heart. In Edmond Rostand's lovely play, *Cyrano de Bergerac*, Cyrano claimed that his true love's name "Roxanne" is like a bell that rings continuously in his heart. Would that Jesus' name rings like that in our hearts. (I'm a romantic.) In honor of today's feast, let us pray, "blessed be the name of Jesus!"

Homily 7

THE PRESENTATION OF JESUS IN THE TEMPLE

"[Jesus'] mother treasured all these things in her heart."

AT THE MEMORIAL SERVICE for the husband of a woman I have known since early childhood, we discussed how even when we were young children our parents let us roam—often not knowing where we were and not worrying. Likewise, Mary and Joseph were happy to travel with their large group without checking whether Jesus was with them. But when it became evident after a few days that Jesus was missing, Mary and Joseph undoubtedly began to worry.

I remember being out in a lightning and thunder storm, pouring rain, gathering night crawlers that I would later use for fishing. I can still see my mother racing up the long road to the farmhouse where I was, deeply upset, for she was deathly afraid of lightning and thunder. Although she scolded me severely, I was having a great time and could not understand why she was so upset. I would be very surprised if anyone here has not seen a panicked mother in a mall or supermarket whose child was missing. Note the fear parents now have allowing their children out, given the shootings and kidnapping in many American cities. In a recent chilling movie, *The Prisoners*, a woman, with her gun pointed at the father who is looking for his missing daughter, explains that after her young son died of cancer, she and her fundamentalist preacher husband went around kidnapping and killing children to turn their parents into demons in order to get even with God. And, she *had* turned this father into a demon who had kidnapped and was torturing in a hidden basement room a person he thought was his daughter's abductor.

The agony of Mary and Joseph searching for three days contrasts sharply with Jesus' calm response when they find him. Mary exclaimed, "How could you do this to us? Your father and I have been looking for you." But Jesus accepts no blame, and indeed issues a gentle rebuke that speaks volumes for his own developing self-awareness. "I have been busying myself with my Father's work." Imagine how Joseph must have felt. And Mary kept all these things in her heart, as did my mother, who related many things to me after my 's death. A mother's heart.

Finding Jesus, of course, will normally involve a surprise. (One friend with five children said that she would have warmed Jesus' bottom—a scene depicted in a fifteenth-century German painting, "The Spanking of Jesus.") Jesus does not do or say what Mary and Joseph were expecting. It is often like that with us too. Many times when we relax and think we have really understood Jesus, he vanishes or shows up where we least expect.

Although Jesus said, "I shall be with you always," how often does he seem absent from our daily, often humdrum, lives? So, we must be prepared to hunt for him, to search for him in prayer, in the Scriptures, in the sacraments, and in each other—and not to give up until we find him again. And discipleship always involves the unexpected.

For example, Mother Teresa wrote that she found the hungry, thirsty, naked, the sick, the abandoned as an unwanted Jesus in his distressing disguise in the slums. Pope Francis learned this lesson when he was Cardinal Archbishop of Buenos Aires. I have found Jesus even in some of my students, but I would not push that too far. "His mother treasured all these things in her heart."

Homily 8

FEAST OF THE HOLY FAMILY

"This child is destined to be a sign of contradiction."

I WAS QUITE STRUCK during a holiday meal when my grandniece remarked: "What a wonderful family we have." Contrast this with the pain caused to a friend whose daughter said during the Thanksgiving dinner: "What's so important about family? We're dysfunctional and most of the time, we stew in each another's juices." A British novelist interviewed on National Public Radio said that what Americans call a dysfunctional family, the British simply call a family. This question is worth asking: What do we as Americans think of when we hear the word *family*? Mother, father, children, even the dog—in short, the nuclear family.

In our Jesuit community there is a very gifted, cosmopolitan African who said that in his culture all the older women and men are called his mothers and fathers and the rest his brothers and sisters. His native tongue has no word for cousin. It amused him when asked at his First Mass by a western Jesuit to meet his mother and father, he pointed to the large group of elderly Africans and said, "These are my mothers and fathers." The holy family?

When thinking of family, I rephrase Winston Churchill's well-known statement: "Family is the worst form of society, except for all those other forms that have been tried from time to time." Although tradition has tended to idealize and romanticize the Holy Family of today's feast, the reality is much different. Look at Jesus' family tree—filled not only with good and upright Jews—and a few good pagans—but also with murderers, thieves, prostitutes, adulterers, and a vile king who even had his own son killed. We are generational beings and we can also find rogues in almost every family tree.

Notice the troubled beginnings of Jesus' family: Joseph observes that Mary, his fiancée, is with child. How would most prospective husbands have understood that? Then to obey the emperor Augustus Caesar's decree, Joseph and Mary are uprooted from their Nazareth home and Jesus is born in Bethlehem and into the human mess. Warned in a dream that king Herod was out to kill the child, (Simeon's prophecy already kicking in that Jesus would be a sign of contradiction), Joseph takes Mary and Jesus to Egypt—like the hunted refugees in so many parts of our contemporary world. Again in a dream, Joseph is ordered to return to Nazareth, where the family would be relatively safe from the whims of tyrants. Jesus is called a Nazarene. The Scriptures ask: "Can anything good come out of Nazareth?"

Soon after the family returned to Nazareth, Joseph died. Unable to care for themselves, Jesus and Mary moved in with relatives. Of course, like those in many parts of the world, the townspeople spoke of Jesus' relatives as his brothers and sisters. When Jesus began his controversial ministry of proclaiming the kingdom of God, this was a direct challenge to the Roman empire that worshipped Caesar as the son of god, as the one who brought peace and justice to the entire known world.

Jesus also spoke of the necessity of hating mother, wife, children, brothers, sisters, and even one's own life. "For I came to set a man against his father, and a daughter against her mother, and a daughter-in-law against her mother-in-law." This radical subverting of family ties must have deeply hurt, shocked, and offended his mother, his so-called brothers and sisters, and the townspeople. Leaving his work as a Nazareth skilled craftsman (he was *not* a carpenter) to become an itinerant preacher of the kingdom of God probably marked him as an uppity local boy. "Is not this the carpenter, the son of Mary and brother of James, Joses, Judas, and Simon, and are not his sisters here with us?" "They took offense at him" and said "he is out of his mind." The Roman governor Festus will later say to the apostle Paul: "You are out of your mind, Paul! Your great learning is driving you mad." Good old family life! I have never done a baptism, marriage, or funeral at which someone was not speaking to someone.

Because of the criticism Jesus received from some of his relatives and the people of his town, he complained that "a prophet is not without honor *except* in his own town, among his relatives, and in his own home. . . ."

and "a person's enemies will be those of his own household." John's Gospel emphasizes that "even his brothers did not believe in him." "And his own received him not." The holy family? Except for Jesus' mother, no relatives were present at the crucifixion. On the cross, Jesus handed his mother over to the care of the Beloved Disciple, not to any family members. However, Jesus' so-called "brothers" were in the upper room for Pentecost—and James, Jesus' so-called brother, became head of the church in Jerusalem.

And yet, because Jesus and Mary are the only persons in history like us in all things *except sin* and because of Joseph's holiness, their family life must have been exceptional. I love the way Mel Gibson's movie, *The Passion of the Christ*, depicts the loving and playful relationship between Jesus and his mother.

So let us rejoice today in our family and community life—imperfect as it might be—by taking to heart the apostle Paul's words in today's second reading: "Put on, as God's chosen ones heartfelt compassion, kindness, humility, gentleness, and patience, bearing with one another and forgiving one another as the Lord has forgiven you, so must you also do. And over all these put on love, that is, the bond of perfection." Only forgiveness and love can fill the cracks of life.

Homily 9

CANA AND MARY

"Do whatever he tells you."

OF EVERYTHING FOUND IN the New Testament, what Jesus' mother says, "do whatever he tells you," is my favorite. When Jesus changed about one-hundred-and-eighty gallons of water into wine and saved the wedding couple from social disgrace, she must have proudly said to the wedding guests, "That's my boy."

During the Advent and Christmas seasons, we heard of Mary as a young engaged woman, undoubtedly looking forward to a normal married family life with Joseph. An angel turned her life upside down, however, when he informed her that "the Holy Spirit will come upon you. The holy one to be born will be called the Son of the Most High." How she must have "pondered all these things in her heart."

Then the pregnant Mary and husband Joseph were forced to travel to Bethlehem because of the whim of some despot. Shepherds came to reverence her son, angels said strange things about him, wise men from the east worshipped her son and gave gifts. How she must have "pondered all these things in her heart." Then Joseph told her that they had to flee to Egypt because the tyrant Herod wanted to kill her son. Later Simeon and Anna spoke of Jesus as the consolation of Israel and that a sword would pierce Mary's soul. Years later Mary and Joseph found Jesus in the Temple and he said curtly that he must be about his Father's business. How she must have "pondered these things in her heart."

CANA AND MARY

When Jesus changed water into wine—the only miracle she witnessed—and when later his actions prompted relatives and neighbors to maintain that he was out of his mind and those in power to claim that he was possessed— how she must have "pondered all these things in her heart." Jesus was arrested, tortured, rejected by his own people, and then sentence to the most shameful death possible for a Jew, "He who hangs upon a tree is cursed." How the pondering in her heart must have taken a different form.

St. Ignatius of Loyola made much of the risen Christ's appearance to his mother. When challenged because this is not in Scripture, he quoted Scripture: "Are you too without understanding?" How all these memories must have come flooding back when Mary was in the cenacle on Pentecost when "they were all filled with the Holy Spirit" (the Spirit of her Son), the same Spirit that descended upon her during the Annunciation. How she must have pondered all these things in her heart.

The apostle Paul wrote simply and laconically of the Virgin Mary: "But when the time had fully come, God sent forth his Son, born of woman." A fairly recent issue of the *National Geographic*, nevertheless, described the Virgin Mary as the world's most powerful woman. Over two-thousand Marian apparitions have been reported since the sixteenth-century: at Lourdes; Jasna Góra in Poland; Kibeho, in Rwanda; Knock in Ireland; Medjugorje in Bosnia-Herzegovina, and so on—rife with miraculous cures and countless spiritual conversions. When at Fatima, I viewed the bullet that felled Pope John Paul II on the Mary statue. Mary has inspired the creation of many of history's great works of art and architecture as well as poetry, liturgy, and music. She is undoubtedly the world's most depicted woman and the spiritual confidante of millions of people, no matter how isolated or forgotten they may be.

One Jewish woman convert wrote that Mary brings us to Jesus, who is the light of the world, just as Jewish mothers light the shabbat candles, and that "we see the relationship of Mary with us isn't just any relationship—it's sacred." Muslims also consider her to be holy above all women. An entire chapter is devoted to her in the Qur'an and her name appears more often there than it does in the Bible.

The image in Mexico of our Lady of Guadalupe is one of the most reproduced female likenesses in history. When Juan Diego, a baptized Aztec peasant—to whom Mary had appeared—opened his cloak to show a skeptical bishop, roses in mid-winter spilled out, revealing the image of our Lady of Guadalupe. This is the only time that Mary is said to have left a painted portrait of herself. This cloak survived an accidental acid spill and also a deliberate bombing by hostile government officials. This cloak is to Mary what the shroud of Turin is to Jesus—an extremely compelling symbol.

According to recent interpretations, an illiterate Aztec would instantly have been able to read the symbols as a nonverbal catechism. The dusky woman's dark hair is parted in the middle, symbolizing that she is a virgin, but she wears a black bow high around her waist, a sign that she is pregnant. Around her neck is a brooch—not the green stone Aztec deities often displayed, but a cross. Her downcast eyes show that she is not a goddess. Similarly, her hands, clasped in prayer, also communicate that she is not divine. One of her legs is bent, suggesting that she could be dancing in prayer. To an Aztec, the turquoise of her cloak signifies divinity and sky. The four-petaled flower in the center of her rose-colored tunic indicates that she is the *God bearer*.

The simple maid of Nazareth is now the world's most powerful woman, reverenced and petitioned by millions. The church proclaims her to be *theotokos*, God-bearer—not only Mary the mother of Jesus but also Mary *the mother of God*. Pope Francis, when once asked what Mary meant to him, answered, "She is my mama." "Do whatever he tells you!"

Homily 10

THE BAPTISM OF THE LORD

"The heavens were opened and the voice of the Father thundered: this is my beloved Son, listen to him."

Baptizing—especially infants and children—has been one of the great joys of my priesthood. When I baptized one of the grandchildren of a man I had taught at Holy Cross College in Worcester, Massachusetts, one of the cousins cried out: "Finn's going tubby." I invited all the children present to stir the water as I blessed it. The grandmother warned me that it was a mistake. It was not.

My fondest memory is of a three-year old whose parents wanted him baptized by total immersion. When I asked if he feared going under water, he said that he loved water and holding his breath under water was fun. So, when his parents took off his clothing and put him in a tub in the sanctuary, I asked him if he were ready. Then I dunked him and baptized him in the name of the Father. As he surfaced, he threw up his hands and yelled "hurrah." The same happened when I baptized him in the name of the Son and of the Holy Spirit. Three hurrahs.

Jesus' baptism is rich in symbolism. It recalls that at the very dawn of creation God's Spirit breathed on the waters, making them the wellspring of all holiness. The waters of the great flood were also made a sign of the waters of baptism, that make an end of sin and a new beginning of holiness. Through the waters of the Red Sea God led Israel out of slavery, to be an image of God's holy people, set free from sin by baptism. In the waters of the Jordan Jesus was baptized by John and anointed with the Holy Spirit.

Water and blood flowed from Jesus' side as he hung upon the cross. After his resurrection Jesus told his disciples to "go out and teach all nations, *baptizing* them in the name of the Father, and of the Son, and of the Holy Spirit." Notice: in the name, *singular,* one God who is Father, Son, and Holy Spirit.

This morning's gospel reminds us that Jesus is the new Moses who crossed the Jordan. Just as Moses had struck the rock to give his people water, Jesus is the rock from which flows living water. One of the gospels underscores John the Baptist's confusion at Jesus' request for his baptism of purification. If anything, John needed to be baptized by Jesus himself. And what happened to John's agenda of fire and brimstone? Jesus humbly identifies himself with God's people by taking their place, living their life, ultimately dying their death. By being baptized, Jesus underscores in yet another powerful way that he has entered into the human mess. God's very Word becoming flesh and dwelling among us is perhaps Christianity's greatest mystery.

I love the trinitarian aspects of Jesus' baptism. God the Father calls Jesus his beloved Son and confirms his mission as the messiah who ushers in God's kingdom. Anointed by the Holy Spirit, he will pour out this Spirit definitively on the cross, in a resurrection appearance, and at Pentecost.

The New Testament defines God the Father in a new way: as the God and Father of our Lord Jesus-Messiah and as the God who raised Jesus from the dead. The Word is God's beloved Son. The Holy Spirit is the Holy Spirit of Jesus-Messiah. As we recall our own baptism, let us ask if our spirituality is trinitarian. Do we pray to the Father as Father, to the Son as Son, to the Holy Spirit as Holy Spirit?

In some parts of the world people celebrate more than their birthdays their baptismal day, their name day, the day on which they became Christians. Do you know the date of your baptism? When some of the great saints sinned, they would immediately recall their baptism, and wash their souls in the water of baptism.

The whole Christian gospel could be summed up this way: that when the living God looks at us who were baptized into Jesus-Messiah's life, death, and resurrection, He says to us what he said to Jesus on that day. He sees us, not as we are in ourselves, but as we are in Christ Jesus. God looks at us and says, "you are my dear, dear child. I'm delighted with you."

"The heavens were opened and the voice of the Father thundered: this is my beloved Son, in whom I am well pleased. Listen to him."

Homily 11

ASH WEDNESDAY AND GENUINE CHRISTIANITY

"Now is the day of salvation."

This morning's readings certainly set the proper tone for Lent: *return* to the Lord with your *whole* heart; we have *sinned*; *now* is the day of salvation; do not be religious *hypocrites*. The influential theologian, H. Richard Niebuhr, wrote that many Christians seek a God without wrath who brought supposed sinless people into a kingdom without judgment through the aid of a Christ without the cross. A recent nationwide survey found that most American young people between the ages of fourteen and twenty-one (I would claim even older) hold what has come to be called a moralistic therapeutic deism. This worldview maintains that a God exists who created, set the world in order, and watches *unobtrusively* over human life. This God wants people to be good, nice, and fair to each other. The central goal of life is to be happy and to feel good about oneself. God does not need to be particularly involved in one's life except when needed to resolve a problem. Finally, good people go to heaven when they die. This is belief in God as the "Divine Butler." "God, please! A little more feeling good in my direction."

This pathetic spirituality is a far cry from true Christianity. I see Lent, therefore, not as a time to give up a favorite dessert, but more as a time to ask oneself in prayer and fasting: What does it really mean to be a Christian? Do you think that king Herod, the Jewish hierarchy, and the Romans sought to kill Jesus-Messiah simply because he wanted everyone to be happy and to be nice to each other?

Jesus teaches that we are to love God with our *whole* hearts, minds, and strength (like Hellman's mayonnaise that uses the entire egg) and to love our neighbor as ourselves, that we cannot be his disciple unless we take up our *cross* daily and follow him—unless we forgive one another seventy-times-seven-times, which, to my mind, is the most difficult thing most people can do.

Jesus also informs us that if we cling to our life we shall lose it and that greater love than this no one has who gives up his life for another. This is hardly the opium of the people ridiculed by Marx or Freud's dismissal of Christianity as a projection of human wants and desires. Who desires the cross, to give up one's life for another, to forgive unceasingly? Jesus likewise exhorts us to be perfect as our heavenly Father is perfect. Does not that mean to grow up, to become a whole human being? Is it true, as one mystic wrote, that most people prefer comfort and entertainment to becoming a whole human being in Jesus-Messiah? Is the late Cardinal Suhard correct when he wrote that the greatest tragedy in life is not to have become a saint? Dying to self for the sake of others brings—not happiness—but joy and peace, and not as the world gives it.

The apostle Paul, who saw the risen Christ on the road to Damascus, wished to know only Christ and him *crucified*. How many of us can endure—even in a small way—what Paul endured to be Jesus-Messiah's disciple: imprisonments; often near death; five times forty lashes less one; three times beaten with rods; almost died from stoning; three times shipwrecked; a night and a day adrift at sea; on frequent journeys; in danger from rivers, from robbers, from his own people, from false brothers, from gentiles; danger in the city, in the wilderness, at sea in toil and hardship, through many a sleepless night, in hunger and thirst, often without food, and in cold and exposure. Does this sound like the life of a Boston college Jesuit professor? One bishop said that wherever Paul went he suffered and caused riots because of his preaching the good news of Jesus-Messiah. The bishop said that wherever he goes, there are cocktail hours and banquets.

The early Christians were called atheists, arrested, tortured, and thrown to the lions in the arena. Why, because their lives reflected that only Jesus crucified and risen is Lord. See how they love one another. Do our Christian lives mirror that in any way? Are we like Annie Hall who said that if the enemy threatened to take away her credit card, she should

ASH WEDNESDAY AND GENUINE CHRISTIANITY

betray even her closest friends? How seriously do we attempt to be mature Christians, say, in matters of concern for the poor, the marginal people of our society, and daily humble love and service? Could we even give up our iPhone, iPad, Facebook, video games, and so on, for even a brief time as a small sign that Jesus is the Lord of our lives? Now is the time of salvation!

In the section of St. Ignatius's *Spiritual Exercises*, where a person is instructed to contemplate the mystery of sin and evil in the light of the crucified Christ, one must ask: What have I done for Christ? Maybe a Lenten sacramental confession is in order? What am I doing for Christ? Almsgiving? Perhaps I should be more like pious Muslims who secretly give away ten percent of their livelihood to the charities of their choice. What will I do for Christ? Let us make that part of our Lent prayer and fasting. *Now* is the time of salvation!

Homily 12

LENT: SATAN TESTS JESUS IN THE DESERT

"At that time Jesus was led by the Spirit into the desert to be tested by the devil."

THIS MORNING'S SCRIPTURAL DUAL between Jesus and Satan reminded me of David James Duncan's terrific novel, *The Brothers K*. In the chapter entitled, "Psalm Wars," a pious mother, who had forced her children to attend Sunday Bible school, is confronted at the dinner table by her now rebellious eldest son. She says, "honor your and mother." He retorts, "unless you hate your mother and your father you cannot be my disciple." And the rather amusing dual continued, with the son clearly winning.

During a pleasant lunch with an old friend a few years ago, we began discussing the hallucinations we had while on pain-killing narcotics after serious surgery. After his spinal surgery, he was on a Stryker frame. Lo and behold: the door to his room would open and horrifying killer cookies, yes cookies—chocolate chip, oatmeal, Orios—would make their way toward him. He would scream and scream until the nurse came. My turn. While recovering from being almost killed in a crosswalk by one of Boston College's cream of the crop football players, I used to awaken in the middle of the night to the assaults of demons so terrifying in their appearance that they made those of the poet-artist William Blake look like bunny rabbits. I wish that I could draw.

When in their grasp, I would mockingly taunt the demons—as Muhammad Ali on the ropes said to George Foreman, with the famous words,

LENT: SATAN TESTS JESUS IN THE DESERT

"Is that all you got, George?," I would pray: "Lord Jesus Christ. Lord Jesus Christ" and say to the demons: "Is that all you got?" Those demons did not stand a chance. When a student asked me if God was testing my faith, I said, "no, Satan is testing out his new demons, a sorry lot!" Why this Christian confidence in the face of the demonic?

In the climax to the most hauntingly beautiful scene in movie history, the agony in the garden of Mel Gibson's *Passion of the Christ*, Jesus arises from his agony victorious—and, with his sandaled heel, crushes the head of the serpent slithering toward him. That is the source of my confidence. Moses and the Israelites had been tested in the desert—but failed. This morning's gospel focuses on Jesus' *testing* (*temptation* is the wrong translation) in the desert—his first routing of Satan. As tester, the devil is probing what sort of son of God, messiah, Jesus is and will be. What sort of Christians are we? Unlike the Israelites in the desert who complained about their hunger—testing God that resulted in the manna from heaven—Jesus states that one must live by God's word, not by bread alone. Jesus is therefore not allowing his personal needs to determine how he will continue to usher in God's kingdom. Jesus' deepest hunger is to do the will of his heavenly Father. That is his meat and drink. What is our deepest hunger?

In challenging Jesus to throw himself down from the Temple, the tester seeks to discover if Jesus will try to accomplish his mission the easy way, that is, by being a wonder-working magician-messiah who will play to the crowds. In challenging Jesus to worship him in order to be given all the world's kingdoms, the tester is again trying to determine if this messiah-Jesus will take the easy way out to free Israel from Roman occupation, rid it of the pseudo-king Herod, and make Israel the superpower to which all the nations of the world will bow—what the Jews, and perhaps even Satan, falsely thought was the kingdom of God. As Jesus will say later to his disciple Peter—who also tried to turn him away from his mission to suffer, die, and be raised—Jesus commands the tester: "Get behind me Satan." What do we really think the kingdom of God is?

Unlike popular views of Jesus as a pious moralizer, "be nice to one another," the New Testament portrays him as the one who does battle to the death with the real enemy of God's kingdom—Satan, the commander-in-chief of a united army of demons—the actual ones behind Israel's sin, the pseudo-king Herod, Pilate, and the Roman occupiers. This morning's gospel underscores that Jesus defeats Satan in their first encounter and later Jesus says: "I saw Satan fall like lightning from heaven." Through his numerous exorcisms, by the Finger of God, the Holy Spirit, he bound the "strong man" and plundered his stronghold. Jesus drove the demons named "legion" out of the Gerasene man, a not so subtle reference to the ones ultimately behind the Roman occupation.

As the one behind the killing of the God-man on the cross and Jesus' descent into hell, Satan thought that he had finally won the battle against Jesus. But Satan overplayed his hand. Some of the early church fathers viewed Jesus as the bait on the hook of the cross, which Satan swallowed to his peril. Scripture proclaims: "Through death Jesus destroyed him who had the power of death, that is, the devil." This statement—and others—reveal the link between sin, death, and ultimately the demonic.

In the Viking TV series, the chieftain Ragnar and his men fail twice to conquer Paris. To the disgust of his men, Ragnar converts to Christianity—under condition that his obsequies and burial be in the cathedral, and that his men be allowed to be present at the city gates. The king and archbishop agree and he is baptized. Shortly thereafter, Ragnar dies, is placed in a coffin, and brought into the Paris cathedral. As the coffin is set down, the very much alive and fully armed Ragnar smashes out of the coffin, thrusts his sword into the archbishop and holds it to the king's throat. The city gates are opened and Paris falls to the Viking victors. A ruse with analogies to the way Christ plundered Satan's stronghold and was raised from the dead as proof of this.

The apostle Paul wrote that Jesus disarmed and made a public spectacle of the demons, triumphing over them by the cross—reversing the Roman symbol of ultimate shame—and the Father raised Jesus from the dead to make him the true Lord of heaven, earth, and even hell. Christianity has long seen life as a spiritual warfare between Jesus and the enemy of our human nature. Sooner or later, we too will encounter Satan and his minions in a variety of forms. Because of the Lord Jesus-Messiah, however, the battle has already been won—but the mopping up action goes on. Let us mop up our lives by praying with St. Ignatius: "What have I done for Christ; what am I doing for Christ; what shall I do for Christ. *Get behind me, Satan.*"

Homily 13

RETHINKING GOOD FRIDAY AND THE CROSS

"My God, my God, why have you forsaken me?"

DURING A DOCTORAL SEMINAR years ago, I was both surprised and disappointed when a priest insisted that Jesus was crucified simply because he was in the wrong place at the wrong time. What nonsense that one of the key elements of our and the world's salvation—history's *central* salvific event —was an accident. As Jesus himself said to the Emmaus disciples, "Did not the Christ have to suffer these things and so enter into his glory?" Besides, of all history's crucified victims, *only* the crucified Jesus-Messiah dominates its memory.

Jesus' claim to be inaugurating the kingdom of God in his *person* was verified by his miraculous cures, exorcisms, raising people from the dead, as well as his predictions against the Temple and the Jewish people. This had made him a key enemy of Jewish authorities. They then demanded that Pontius Pilate execute Jesus by crucifixion. Just as one of the goals of Nazi Germany was to turn the Jewish people into excrement, Roman crucifixion was structured to turn their worst enemies into excrement. And because the Book of Deuteronomy proclaims that he who hangs upon a tree is cursed, Jewish eyes would have viewed the crucified Jesus-Messiah as excrement cursed by God.

The Romans had perfected one of the most gruesome forms of execution ever invented. The Roman soldiers would have delighted in scourging a naked victim with whips that tore flesh from his back and buttocks and then sexually abusing this Jewish circumcised prisoner throughout the night. Then, crowned with thorns and donning a purple robe, Jesus the king would have been ridiculed, taunted, mocked, and spit upon: a ritual of total infamy. These soldiers were highly skilled at driving the nails just close enough to the radial nerves to cause violent bolts of pain when the cross was lifted, and whenever the victim attempted to move. Because the crucified could breathe only if he moved—thus intensifying his pain—in a sense, he killed himself by suffocation. Besides, the unspeakably thirsty crucified person was usually naked, unable to control bodily functions, and tormented by carrion birds and insects feasting on open wounds—all adding to his humiliation and suffering. This excruciation could last several days. The crucified were purposely made a public spectacle, a billboard, a sign warning, "do not mess with the Romans." Exposed to the full scorn of spectators, Jesus would have been subjected to their verbal abuse and to their throwing of whatever objects and filth were at hand. Death by crucifixion was so vile and horrendous that it was against the law to crucify a Roman citizen. Even the word was not uttered in polite Roman society. Because of the teaching in the Book of Deuteronomy that he who hangs upon a tree is cursed, Jews would have found crucifixion even more abhorrent because of its association with God's *curse*.

Jesus-Messiah crucified: a pitiable, twisted, contorted, shuddering of the God-man, a comic gargoyle, the suffering servant prophesied by Isaiah and Psalm 22:6: "I am a worm and no man." Jesus' cry of dereliction on the cross, "My God, my God, why have you forsaken me," indicates the depths of his suffering. Christianity's supreme paradox: the all holy *God*-man is not only cursed by God, but in the words of the apostle Paul, God made him who had no sin to be sin for us. God curses the *God*-man? The *God*-man becomes sin? How the apostle Paul and the early Christians must have been ridiculed when they preached a *crucified* messiah. This is behind the apostle Paul's strange words that he was not ashamed to preach the gospel of Jesus-Messiah crucified.

In an excellent book on the life of Christ, Archbishop Alban Goodier wrestled with the question of how Jesus' limited, finite sufferings were the source of the world's salvation. He focused, however, only on the Jesus' human physical and psychological sufferings. The crucifixion underscores that *God himself* not only suffered, was tortured, bled, and died for our sins but also became sin itself. As the second-century bishop, Melito of Sardis, proclaimed: "He was raised on the cross. He who fixed the heavens is fixed to the wood. *God is murdered!*"

The Qur'an simply denies that Jesus was crucified because the notion that God would have done something so atrocious to a great prophet is simply unthinkable. The Aztec king Montezuma asked the Spanish conquistador, Cortez, why the Son of God was sacrificed when he should have been the one to whom sacrifice was given. I applaud the pastor who upset his parishioners because he placed a statue of Jesus in an electric chair in the parish church. Still, even the electric chair is a far cry from history's most vile and revolting instrument of death, the cross. Have we not domesticated the cross, made it routine and respectable? This subversive symbol is so paradoxical that Madonna uses it in her shows. Rock stars, celebrities, and ordinary people wear and display it as non-religious jewelry.

Although the apostle Paul had encountered the *risen* Christ on the Damascus road, he proclaims unashamedly that he now wants only to know Jesus-Messiah *crucified*. Popular opinion notwithstanding, there is no genuine Christianity without the cross. Christ says it clearly: "Whoever wants to be my disciple must deny himself and take up his cross daily and follow me."

Homily 14

RETHINKING GOOD FRIDAY AS CHRIST'S DESCENT INTO HELL

"I have the keys of Death and Hades."

CHRIST CRUCIFIED HAS BEEN called a super-saturated phenomenon, that is, one with inexhaustible meaning. As a result, I wish to emphasize only two aspects of history's most important event. First, God made Jesus—who had no sin—to be sin for us. In addition, according to the Book of Deuteronomy, he who hangs upon a tree is cursed. Thus, the sheer Godlessness and horror of the cross—Jesus' cursed and sin itself—seemingly utterly defeated. Satanic evil and our evil murder the way, the truth, and the life—the *God*-man himself.

Second, the cross is where the *victorious* Jesus-Messiah descended into hell, the realm of Godlessness, and conquered Satan, sin, and death in an apocalyptic battle that fully reveals the triumph of the trinitarian God's love for us. The Christian paradox: victory though defeat; resurrected life through a gruesome death. Love replaced hate.

In the *Viking* TV series, the chieftain Ragnar and his men fail twice to conquer Paris. To his men's disgust, Ragnar converts to Christianity—under condition that when he dies, his obsequies and burial be in the cathedral, and that his men be allowed to be present at the city gates. With the king and the archbishop agreeing to these terms, Ragnar is baptized. Shortly thereafter, he dies, is placed in a coffin, and brought into the Paris cathedral. As the coffin is set down, the fully armed and much alive Ragnar smashes out of the coffin, thrusts his sword into the archbishop and then holds it to the king's throat. The city gates are opened and Paris falls to the Vikings. A brilliant ruse and one I see as faintly analogous to Christ's death on the cross as an aspect of his descent into hell. Jesus-Messiah's descent into hell is a symbolic narrative that affirms what happened on the cross: his final and definitive exorcism. Christ had predicted that he would enter and plunder the strong man's house, bind him, and carry off his possessions.

The apostle Paul proclaims that on the cross, the conquering Christ disarmed the principalities and powers and made them a public spectacle. In John's Gospel, Jesus predicts that when he is lifted up, he will draw all to himself. And as the Epistle to the Hebrews proclaims, "Since the children have flesh and blood, he too shared in their humanity so that by his death he might break the power of him who holds the power of death—that is, the devil—and free those who all their lives were held in slavery by their fear of death." Thus, it is easy to understand why the early Christians made Christ's *triumphant* descent into hell on the cross the centerpiece of their faith—and why they considered Holy Saturday as an aspect of Good Friday.

Scripture makes it clear that God's Word became flesh in order to invade the kingdom ruled by SATAN, SIN, AND DEATH—all in capital letters. In short, it was Christ's kingdom versus Satan's kingdom. The paradox: the apocalyptic war between two kingdoms and two Lords was waged by the sinless God-man who became sin and endured both the shame and curse of the cross. *God became sin? God cursed God?* Why? To use Satan's very weapons against Satan—on our behalf and for our sins. Some early church fathers viewed Christ as the bait on the Father's fish hook that Satan swallowed—to his downfall. A more contemporary version: A Christian should view Christ's death on the cross, his descent into hell, as his *cosmic conquest*. In this way, he negated the power of Satan, sin, and death over *all God's creation*. Think about Luke Skywalker of the *Star Wars* movies who flew his X-wing fighter into the heart of the death star and destroyed it.

Scripture proclaims that Christ descended to the lower, earthly regions and after being made alive, proclaimed the gospel both to imprisoned spirits and the dead. Contemporary liberation theologians maintain that Jesus' baptism indicates his solidarity and identification with all humanity. They also opine that Jesus' descent into hell underscores his solidarity with the dead, the forgotten, the victims of tyranny, slavery, injustice—the utterly silent and forgotten of history.

I go even further. The descent into hell underscores the complete solidarity of Jesus-Messiah with us in sin and death. The dead Jesus sank into a pit of blackness so profound that no light of hope could reach it. Utterly cut off from his powers, seemingly abandoned by his, devoid of any hope of redemption or victory—precisely in this total emptying, he brought his solidarity with us and with our lot to its climax. The *crucified, cursed-made-sin God*-man Jesus-Messiah suffered not only the common death of a criminal but also what the Book of Revelation calls the *second death*, the descent into hell. The invading, plundering, binding, warrior Christ, in blazing white, strides triumphantly over the shattered gates of hell. Sheer majesty and dominion, the triumphant expedition of the victorious Christ the king depicted in many artistic works, known as the harrowing of hell. Jesus descended into hell, moreover, to destroy the power of Satan, sin, and death over all God's creation. This includes not only people past, present, and future—the Godly *and* the ungodly—but also the entire creation.

Did not the apostle Paul write: "*Creation* itself will be set free from its bondage to decay and obtain the glorious liberty of the children of God. We know that *the whole creation* has been groaning in travail together until now." How many Christians realize the cosmic nature of Jesus-Messiah's death on the cross and his descent into hell? Jesus' apocalyptic victory reached and transformed every dimension of creation: earth, heaven, and even hell—all this by Christ making peace by the blood of his cross.

As one theologian boldly wrote: "Hell will now be seen not as an evil, but as the place where those who reject Christ are still cared for by Christ—and not simply as Lord and judge but as savior and healer. The triune God will punish transgressions, but will not remove from us his steadfast love or be false to his faithfulness." As Jesus says in the Book of Revelation: "I have the keys of Death and Hades."

Homily 15

RESURRECTION: IN NO OTHER NAME

"Then the Beloved Disciple said to Peter, "it is the Lord!"

I WELCOME YOU TO our Easter season celebration. Johannes Roothaan, the superior general who rebuilt the Society of Jesus after its restoration in 1814, cautioned against often meditating and contemplating the resurrection because it leads to laxity. In contrast, a fifteenth-century Flemish Beguine-mystic rightly urged profound contemplation of the *glorified wounds of* and the imitation of the *risen* Christ—a highly unusual view in the spiritual tradition.

The bodily resurrection of Jesus Christ has been underscored as God the Father's mightiest deed, the unique and sensational event on which the whole of human history turns. In fact, the New Testament defines God in a new way, as the God who raised Jesus from the dead. When St. Peter cured a man lame from birth, he said, "in the *name of Jesus* of Nazareth, walk. He then explained that he cured this man through the risen Christ. "In no other name."

Today's gospel centers on Jesus' appearance to the disciples at the sea of Tiberias. The Beloved Disciple is the first to recognize Jesus: "It is the Lord." Nonetheless, Peter, splash, is the first in the water to swim to shore. One-hundred-fifty-three large fish had been caught. The one-hundred-fifty-three is not a symbolic number, as St. Augustine held, but an eyewitness account of the actual catch. No extra charge.

Years ago I received a frantic phone call from a Jesuit who was to give ten lectures on Christian mysticism in Jerusalem at an inter-religious dialogue but had to go in for emergency heart surgery. After he had forwarded his lecture outlines, I asked him why they were all centered on abstract mysticism. He replied that the audience of Hindus, Buddhist, Jews, Muslims, and New Age pagans would not want the name Jesus Christ mentioned. I said to myself: "Hmm, a Jesuit unwilling to speak of Jesus Christ. I thought of the German theologian Karl Rahner who would never water down his Catholicism in the interests of either ecumenical or interreligious dialogue. I went to Jerusalem and gave my lectures as one who worships the crucified and *risen* Lord, Jesus Christ. Not surprisingly, they were well received. Anyone interested in true intra-religious dialogue has no desire to hear a bowdlerized version of another's real position. "In no other name." "It is the Lord."

When teaching at Santa Clara University many years ago, I befriended a young Buddhist priest, pastor of a Buddhist parish in Los Gatos. He told me that curious Christians often visited and asked what he thought about Christianity. He told them that Christianity's foundation is the person of Jesus Christ who is confessed and worshipped as the crucified and risen God-man. Although not a believer, this Buddhist priest gave a reply that I wish more Christians were capable of giving. "In no other name." "It is the Lord."

Shortly before his death, the atheist, Christopher Hitchens, spoke of Jesus Christ as a madman, a megalomaniac, who allegedly thought that he was the way, the truth, and the life. I liked what Hitchens said because he read the New Testament correctly. Jesus' incredible claims could come in no way from simply a teacher, a prophet, a Buddha, a philosopher, or any of history's religious geniuses. I give Hitchens credit for understanding what he was rejecting. "In no other name." "It is the Lord."

The God who raised Jesus from the dead confirms that Jesus is who and what he said he was: the Messiah, the Lord, the Son of Man, the last Adam, the life-giving Spirit, the seed of the new creation, the kingdom incarnate—the way, the truth and the life. The entire New Testament is written in the light of the risen Christ. The truth of the bodily resurrection of Jesus-Messiah is not simply one truth among others to believe. It is the very reason to believe. "In no other name." "It is the Lord."

During an ecumenical seminar in Germany, the Jesuit theologian Karl Rahner startled many of the participants and his audience when he said that "you really cannot do Christology unless, like the Beloved Disciple, you have quickly recognized him as Lord, and, like Peter, plunged into the

RESURRECTION: IN NO OTHER NAME

sea of life to reach him, fallen in love with him, and thrown your arms around him." One theologian interjected: "As long as you do not mean that piously." Rahner: "I mean it the way it sounds." "In no other name." "It is the Lord."

The bodily resurrection of Jesus Christ is the sign not only that I shall be raised from the dead but also that we shall be raised from the dead, that creation itself shall be raised as the new earth and new heaven—that forgiveness, healing, and transformation—not sin and death—have the last word because the risen Christ is the 's definitive word of love. "In no other name." "It is the Lord."

Homily 16

JESUS' EASTER APPEARANCES

"We have seen the Lord . . . . My Lord and my God."

A WOMAN I KNOW woke out of a sound sleep to find her younger brother-in-law at the foot of her bed. Joyriding and trying to beat a train with his car to the crossing, he had been killed a few weeks before. He asked the woman why she had never liked him. She replied: "I never really knew you." He said, "all right," and never returned. She never told her husband. A good example of what psychologists call a bereavement experience. Years ago, a Scandinavian girl was pronounced clinically dead on the operating table—but later revived. She told the hospital staff and her parents that she had been in heaven and met Jesus. Because she was a skilled artist, she drew his picture. Years later, an American boy was also pronounced clinically dead on the operating table, but later revived. He, too, said that he had been in heaven and saw Jesus. His minister showed him his collection of Jesus images. The boy picked out the one the Scandinavian girl had painted. You can google this.

When teaching years ago at lovely Santa Clara University in California, I befriended the widowed mother of one of my students. She told me that shortly after her husband died, he would appear to her at different times and places in their home. This happened for weeks. Finally, when her deceased husband appeared again, she said to him, "listen, we had a good marriage, a good life with terrific children and grandchildren. I took care of you for years when you were sick. Now go in peace and leave me

JESUS' EASTER APPEARANCES

alone." He never appeared again. Another example of what psychologists call a bereavement experience.

In Tom Hanks's film, *Cast Away*, a FedEx systems analyst finds himself on an uninhabited island in the Pacific southwest—the sole survivor of a plane crash caused by a storm and the explosion of dangerous cargo. Presumed dead by his co-workers, family, and fiancée, Hanks manages to be rescued after four years of survivor living. When his former fiancée—now with a husband and young daughter—learns by phone that he is alive, she faints. During a company party in Hanks's honor, his boss says: "Now we must bring you back to life again."

In this morning's gospel, we find something entirely different: Jesus' disciples are behind locked doors—full of fear that maybe they will soon face the same horrible death by crucifixion their master did. Moreover, there are rumors that Jesus' tomb is empty and that women have been told strange things by angels. The night is dark and full of terror! Even more startling, the very Jesus who was crucified and entombed, later stands before them and shows them his wounded hands and side. Jesus then bestows his messianic peace upon them, *Shalom*, which, for a Jew, meant the *fullness of human well-being*—both spiritual and physical.

Just as Jesus had washed their feet, he now breathes his Holy Spirit, the Spirit of Pentecost, upon them—just as God did when he breathe into the dust of the earth and created Adam. His disciples become the new Adam transformed by Jesus' Holy Spirit and are given the ability to forgive sins! "Who can forgive sins except God alone?" Perhaps so overcome with grief, Thomas the Twin was not with them—or, he was out scouting the area for danger. He was the disciple who had previously said, "let us go and die with him," but now refuses to believe unless he can put his finger and hand into Jesus' wounds.

Again, on yet another Sunday, the Lord's day, Jesus appears. Notice—instead of scolding them for abandoning him—"where were *you* after the soldiers took me away? You weren't even present at my death"—Jesus again bestows his messianic peace upon them and commands Thomas: "All right, put your finger into my glorious wounds. No ghost here! Remember when my Father kicked Adam and Eve out of the garden lest they stretch out their hand and eat of the tree of life? Stretch out your hand into my glorious open side—unlike your locked doors—and enter the gate of immortal life, the new creation, the new Temple, of my risen body." Despite doubting Thomas's reputation, he utters the profoundest confession of faith in the entire Scriptures: "My Lord and my God." This is Christianity's foundation: the person of Jesus Christ, confessed and worshipped as the crucified and risen God-man. If someone asks you what Christianity is, this is it. *My Lord*: neither Caesar, nor Herod, nor the Caesars to come, nor the Buddha, nor Krishna, nor Obama, nor Hillary, nor Trump, nor Putin is Lord—a confession of faith that has profound political ramifications and resulted in the deaths of so many Christians to this day who refused to acknowledge other so-called lords.

My God. My niece's family adopted a very bright beagle-basset mix, "Hazel," who already knows a number of tricks. Supposing one day she began to speak English, to read and write, to discuss politics. One would ask: What do have we here? This happened to the disciples. They undoubtedly followed Jesus because they thought him to be a prophet, a teacher, even the promised Messiah—but Jesus kept raising the ante. What prophet would have dared to forgive sins, to place his law above what God had commanded the Jews through Moses concerning murder, adultery, retaliation, etc.? "You have heard it said of old. God said but I say to you." What prophet would have claimed to be greater than the Temple, than Solomon, than Jonah? What prophet would have claimed that he and the Father were one, that only he had seen the Father, that he who sees him sees the Father, and that salvation comes only through him? And they eventually worshipped this man as God—an incredible step for a Jew! "We have seen the Lord. . . . My Lord and my God."

Homily 17

FEAST OF JESUS' BODY AND BLOOD

"Take! Eat and drink: this is my body and blood."

THIS MORNING'S READINGS FOR the feast of the solemnity of the most holy Body and Blood of Christ offer an unusually good summary of the Last Supper, Good Friday, Easter, and Ascension. The Word became flesh, body and blood, and dwelt among us—in the full sense of that phrase. In John's First Letter, we read: "We have heard, seen, and touched the word of life." Jesus said to Thomas: "Put your finger here; see my hands. Reach out your hand and put it into my side. Stop doubting and believe." The incarnation, the Word became flesh, Jesus' bodily resurrection, the flesh is the hinge of salvation—what could be more central to genuine Christianity.

This feast also sums up what I recently told someone who claimed that blood transfusions are a grave sin. Jesus himself said: "Unless you eat my body and drink my blood you have no life in you." It reminds me, too, that many Catholics put up with so much imperfection and sin in the church because of their love of the Mass in which they receive Christ's Body and Blood.

It is obvious that we are body-persons and that we do bleed. Do we not admire those who put their bodies on the line to protect us: the military, the police, firemen, doctors without borders, health care workers, and so many others, too numerous to list? Jesus, "he loved us and gave himself for us"—body and blood. Julian of Norwich the fourteenth to fifteenth century mystic maintain that blood was love made visible.

HOMILIES IN A NEW KEY

The body is the temple of the Holy Spirit. The elegance and grace of ballet, Flamenco, Olympic gymnastics. The body: the imposing beauty of Michelangelo's and August Rodin's sculptures. Arnold Schwarzenegger in his prime or Serena Williams. The enjoyment of good food and drink; the joy of dancing—ever see the Japanese film, *Shall We Dance*, which is better than the Fred Astaire and Ginger Rogers version? The joy of sports at their best, deflated football or not. Tom Brady's nine Super Bowl wins. Many Chinese youths can name several American basketball players, but not the president of the United States. And few things brighten my day more than to see a young mother pushing her baby in a jogging stroller with her trusty dog running alongside.

The body: intimacy. Another Jesuit and I performed the wedding liturgy for a young woman we both had taught. He refused to say the prayer: "Lord, be as close to us as the body of the other." I prayed it. In the Jane Fonda-Robert Redford movie, *Our Souls at Night*, the elderly woman widow invites the elderly widowed man to spend the night with her—not for anything sexual—but for the intimate bed conversion she so missed since her husband died. The human need for intimacy. Years ago I taught a young woman who was quite struck by another Jesuit's advice to students: Find a *sacramental* mate, one who will lead you more deeply into God's mystery. She told me years later that every time she and her husband conjoined, she would say: "This is my body." The body, the gift of self, intimacy and love. "Body of Christ, save me; Blood of Christ, inebriate me," phrases from a prayer dear to St. Ignatius of Loyola.

Contrast this with the promiscuous young woman whose mother complained about her sleeping around. "I am just giving my body now," she said, "but when I meet the right person, I will give my entire self." Nice try! Another woman sadly related to me recently that her husband was highly sexual but totally lacking in affection. I'm convinced that he is unfaithful. Another young woman said that she does not care what people do with their bodies—to which I replied: "I wish that your parents had thought of that."

These events brought to mind the utterly beautiful, holy, and chaste wedding night eroticism depicted in Italian director Franco Zeffirelli's film, *Romeo and Juliet*. In C. S. Lewis's amusing and instructive book, *The Screwtape letters*, the demon uncle writes to his demon nephew about the disgust he has for chaste virgins who marry and then give themselves joyfully and unreservedly to their husbands. Why? Because God has blessed

FEAST OF JESUS' BODY AND BLOOD

such a union. The first blessing in the Bible is on man and wife. Does not chaste sexual union symbolize Christ's union with and love of his church?

One of the best ways to understand Jesus' Passover meal with his disciples, the bloody sacrifice on the cross, and the sacrificial meal of the Mass is to focus on the blood of the Jewish peace offering, the blood of the Sinai covenant, described in this morning's first reading. Blood is a symbol of life. Pouring the blood on the altar—where heaven and earth meet—symbolizes that all life belongs to God. The blood is then sprinkled on the people to dramatize that life is God's gift to us and a symbol of the one blood, the one life, shared between God and his people. Notice: there is no angry pagan God in a Jewish peace offering.

We've all seen movies in which two men slit their hand to mingle blood to become blood brothers. In the movie, *The Indian Runner*, a small town sheriff tracks down in a bar his deeply troubled and violent Vietnam veteran brother. The good brother breaks a beer bottle and slits the palm of his hand, blood, and tells his violent brother: "See the family blood here. Come home or stay in the hell of this bar with your drunkenness." In the movie, *The Red Violin*, the wife of the violin makes dies before he finishes his masterpiece. He drains her blood and stains the violin with it. In the Netflix series, *Ertugrul: Resurrection*, the evil Mongol chief slits his palm, his trusted men do the same, he squeezes his blood into a cup, passes it around, the men do the same, and then he drinks the blood. A symbol of blood unity.

The apostle Paul writes of "the church of God that [Jesus] acquired with his own *blood*." The fourteenth-century mystic saint and doctor of the church, Catherine of Siena, exhorts her readers to drown in "the blood and fire pouring from Jesus' pierced side." Our fourth floor chapel has a lovely hand-carved wooden pelican on the door. The pelican, an ancient symbol of Christ, was believed to wound itself in order to feed its young with its own blood. In one of St. Thomas Aquinas's hymns, he implores Jesus: "Pelican of mercy, cleanse me in thy precious blood."

The apostle Paul exhorts us: "In view of God's mercy, offer your bodies as a living sacrifice, holy and pleasing to God—this is your true and proper worship." Baptized into Christ's death and resurrection, we are now Jesus' body and blood, called to fill up what is lacking in Christ's sufferings through the suffering, love, and forgiveness demanded of us in our often humdrum, daily lives. "Body of Christ, save me; Blood of Christ, inebriate me."

Homily 18

RETHINKING BLOOD SACRIFICE

"This is the Blood of the Covenant."

THIS MORNING'S FIRST READING focuses on the blood of the Sinai covenant. As I have said in many homilies, I maintain that the blood of the Jewish peace offering is the best way to understand Jesus' bloody sacrifice on the cross and the sacrifice of the Mass. Blood is a symbol of life. For many mystics, blood is love made visible. Pouring the blood on the altar—where heaven and earth meet—symbolizes that all life belongs to God. The blood is then sprinkled on the people to dramatize that life is God's gift to us. It also symbolizes the one blood, the one life, shared between God and his people. We've all seen movies in which two men slit their hand to mingle blood to become blood brothers. Please take note, too, that there is no wrathful pagan God in a Jewish peace offering.

A Catholic church, in a charming Austrian village contains a striking mural that depicts Jesus restraining the sword arm of the wrathful God the Father—with Mary holding up her mantel of protection with the world and its people behind. What is your image of God the Father? What was the Father's will with respect to Jesus' sacrifice on the cross and thus the meaning of the sacrifice of the Mass? "This is the blood of the covenant."

Many Christians to this day believe that when Adam and Eve sinned, they had equivalently spit in God's face, an infinite offense. God the Father became angry, wrathful, and closed the gates of heaven. Sinful humans are incapable of paying back an infinite debt. The solution, Jesus, the God-man who as God can pay off an infinite debt and as man pays the debt incurred by human sin through his bloody sacrifice that placates a wrathful God from dooming us all.

This view may be good Calvinism that Christ was punished instead of us but it is definitely not good Catholicism. The great fourteenth to fifteenth century mystic, Julian of Norwich, wrote that a Trinity of love cannot be wrathful. How can a just God, a God who *is Love* demand the murder of his innocent Son? Isn't this child abuse in its most extreme form?

An analogy: During the Chernobyl nuclear disaster, a Russian air force general sent his helicopter pilot son into harm's way. The pilots who covered the reactor with sand and cement faced certain death from radiation. That Russian general, a father, certainly did not want his son to die—but to save others. Likewise, God the willed Jesus beautiful, noble, authentic human life to conquer Satan and evil. Is it not the Father who sacrificed his Son out of love for us? God so loved the world that he gave us his only son. Did not Christ sacrifice himself to carry out the Father's will that Satan and evil be defeated? Thus, I reject any view of the cross that Christ was punished in our stead. One might say that since Christ became sin, God punished *sin*, but not Jesus himself. I understand the cross as the supreme symbol both of God's love for humanity and of the definitive exorcism that renders the principalities and powers ultimately impotent. Without the cross, authentic humanism cannot exist.

In the fourth-century before Christ, Plato wrote: "The perfectly just man will have to be scourged, racked, fettered, blinded, and then after the most extreme suffering, he will be crucified." One twentieth-century Dominican theologian, Herbert McCabe, wrote that "if you love effectively, you will be killed." Why? In the face of holiness, one must either change, be converted, or murder holiness. When Peter first met Jesus, he cried out, "depart from me for I am a sinful man." Were not Gandhi and Martin Luther King assassinated because of their courage to challenge evil?

Jesus is the human face of eternal Love whose life, death, and resurrection reveal that there is something *in us* that hates God. Sin. The blood of the cross proclaims that God loves us despite our hatred of him. It also shows the power of evil, of Satan, of the principalities and powers, of the human heart that are all willing to kill the way, the truth, and the life. Jesus' bloody sacrifice and also the Mass as a sacrificial meal are the Father's gift to us, a symbol of total giving of oneself. God's blood and our blood; God's life and our life. "This is the blood of the covenant."

Homily 19

EATING AND DRINKING CHRIST'S FLESH AND BLOOD

"Unless you eat the flesh of the son of man and drink his blood, you have no life in you."

As I grow in age and rage, the fault of my teenage years that most troubles me is the selfish way I took for granted the sacrifices my father and mother made to raise and educate me. Whenever I spoke to my students of having drunk the blood of my father and mother in an egotistical way, I always sensed that I had awakened some students to the embarrassing realization that they, too, were guilty of the same narcissism.

One of the most moving stories about King David concerns the time when he and his fighting men were pinned down by the Philistines who were occupying his native town of Bethlehem. Because of increasing thirst, King David said out loud how much he would like to have water from the Bethlehem well. Three of his best fighting men broke through the Philistine army lines, and brought back Bethlehem well-water for David.

But David poured the water on the ground and said: "God forbid that I should drink the blood of these men who risked their lives for me." David was too shrewd to be seen profiting from his men's courage, a selfishness that he compared to the drinking their blood. Jesus, however, commands his followers to drink his blood. Jesus says essentially, "if you want to profit from what I am doing, you must eat my flesh and drink my blood." Like King David, however, Jesus refuses to drink the blood of his disciples, that is, to profit from the risk of their lives. Jesus, as the true messiah, will put his

EATING AND DRINKING CHRIST'S FLESH AND BLOOD

own life on the line and actually lose it. His disciples will profit from Jesus' death through a promised resurrection and eternal life.

The gospel readings of the past few weeks centered on physical hunger that Jesus satisfied by multiplying the loaves and fish for over five-thousand people. In so doing, he underscored that the kingdom of God he both is and inaugurates by his presence is a kingdom very much concerned with *this world*—with human beings and their needs. But the first reading turns our attention to the spiritual hunger and thirst of human beings. God's Wisdom commands us to eat of her food and drink of her wine—not in the false way that Adam and Eve ate the fruit from the tree of the knowledge of good and evil—and were therefore barred from eating the fruit from the tree of life. To know the meaning of life and to live accordingly is true wisdom. Jesus, God's enfleshed Wisdom, prayed: "That they know you, the only true God, and Jesus Christ, whom you have sent." The apostle Paul scoffed at Greek wisdom and emphasized that only Jesus crucified and risen is God's true wisdom. And Jesus promised wisdom, eternal life, to those who eat his flesh and drink his blood. As the bread from heaven, Jesus is the new tree of life. Only eating from this tree quenches our spiritual hunger and thirst. Is there anything more shrouded in mystery in our daily experience than the process of nutrition, the transformation of a variety of foods into human living bodily tissue—we who are made in God's image and likeness. Imagine, something as simple as an apple transformed into something human.

This morning's gospel of course refers to the Eucharist, the Lord's supper, the sacrament at which Jesus mysteriously gives us his body and blood to be eaten and drunk. In this way, we become Jesus' mystical body, truly changed into and united with him. As the apostle Paul writes: "Since there is one bread, we who are many are one body; for we all partake of the one bread." The nutritional process is reversed: Instead of food becoming us, we become the body and blood of Christ we eat and drink.

Human eating and drinking does more than nourish us. I love to cook. I've done Christmas Eve pasta meals for at least the past thirty-five years that family and friends rave about. I even cooked elk last Christmas. At the former apartment building, I had my own kitchen and loved to cook Indian, Korean, Chinese, Malaysian, and other spicy foods for those who appreciated tasty food. I've noticed over the years how good food and drink deepens family life, binds friends more deeply together, and creates community.

Is this not what Jesus many meals with his disciples, his emphasis on the messianic banquet in the age to come, the Last Supper, the Eucharist, symbolize? When thrown to the lions in the arena, the saint and martyr Ignatius of Antioch cried out,: "I am God's wheat, ground fine by the lion's teeth to be made the purest bread for Christ." The Eucharist we celebrate in remembrance of Christ asks us to be martyred daily for others. Being a good priest is like being nibbled to death by pollywogs. Marriage, raising children, single life—daily life for most people is no different. Few of us will be thrown to the lions, but Christ asks all Christians to be thrown in self-sacrificing love to the pollywogs that inflict the martyrdom of daily life.

Homily 20

RETHINKING JESUS' ASCENSION

"Then what if you were to see the son of man ascend to where he was before!"

THE SCRIPTURES MAKE NUMEROUS references to Jesus' ascension into glory and sitting at the Father's right hand. Well known, of course, is the Old Testament depiction of Elijah's ascension into heaven in a fiery chariot. Please keep your eye on the nearby reservoir during evenings. If you see a blazing fiery red Lamborghini with black leather seats ascending, you can say, "there goes Egan."

Ascension does not mean space travel, with Jesus as the first cosmonaut. Ascension is simply the symbolic way New Testament writers underscore Jesus passage from this visible, tangible world to the invisible world of his Father. Ascension likewise emphasizes the eternal significance of his *humanity*. Jesus did not turn into a ghost. Ascension is also another way of emphasizing that his resurrection appearances have ended. "Blessed are those who have not seen yet believe." As well, ascension underscores Jesus' glorification, his getting up in the world, his sitting at the Father's right hand, his being Lord of heaven, earth, and the underworld. Not only because Jesus is God's holiness and love incarnate but also because he fulfilled his Father's will to defeat Satan and to usher in God's kingdom through his life, death, and resurrection, does his glorious ascension stress his inner worth that commands respect and esteem. Lift up your hearts.

How deeply embedded in human nature is our desire for "getting up in the world," for glory. Several years ago the *Boston Globe* had photos of and an article on Boston University's president John Silber's exclusive penthouse office—high up in the world, overlooking the city. It was contrasted with Boston College president J. Donald Monan's lowly, little house office on the prairie of Old Colony Road. Two university presidents with much different styles. Getting up in the world—glory.

Why did the United Arab Emirates construct the Khalifa skyscraper so high that about twenty-five percent of its floors are above the clouds? The Taipei world finance center and the Petronas twin towers in Malaysia are almost as high—and dwarf Chicago's Sears tower and the Empire State building. Getting up in the world—glory. Early in the Scriptures we find people who say: "Let us build ourselves a tower that reaches to the heavens, so that we may make a name for ourselves." The tower of Babel, getting up in the world, glory, making a name for oneself. Some things never change.

I often think how intoxicating it must be for famous people to have their names in lights, to be referred to frequently in the media. Is there not anything like praise, hearing one's name mentioned, seeing one's name in the newspapers, or elsewhere—how exciting! Even more paradoxical: What did the serpent offer Adam? To be like God. The first temptation: to be like God, up in the world, determining what is good and what is evil. Glory! The tragic Santa Barbara shooter who said: "I shall be a god."

Jesus turns all this on its head. The apostle Paul writes, "Jesus, who, being in very nature God, did not cling to his equality with God, but made himself nothing, taking the very nature of a servant, became man, humbled himself, and became obedient to death, even death on a cross." And, as mentioned, the most shameful death possible for a Jew because, as Scripture proclaims, he who hangs upon a tree is cursed by God.

Not only that. Quite striking and mysterious, God the Father made the sinless Jesus to be sin for us so that we might become God's righteousness. Moreover, Jesus descended into hell itself. Therefore God the Father exalted him to the highest place and gave him the name that is above every name, that at the name of Jesus every knee should bend, in heaven and on earth and under the earth, and every tongue confess that Jesus Christ is Lord, to the glory of God the Father. That is the true meaning of Jesus' ascension and glorification. The Christian paradox: there is no glory without first enduring the curse of the cross, becoming sin, and descending into hell.

Finally, I wish to call attention to the ascension's political dimension. If Jesus is King of kings and Lord of lords, then the pretensions of pseudo-king Herod, the first person to seek Jesus' death, and of Caesar Augustus are bogus. And within a generation, Jesus' followers would be persecuted by the Roman empire for refusing to acknowledge Caesar as Lord. In addition, Christians who proclaimed Jesus as Lord were persecuted by later empires, large and small, as we find with ISIS and other brutes in our own day. What nonsense that Christianity is a private matter that has nothing to do with politics. Jesus was a first-century Judean Jew whose central message focused on the kingdom of God—not universal love—as one often hears. And, the kingdom of God is very much of *this world*, with strong political overtones. Jesus did *not* say "my kingdom is not of this world," but my kingdom is not *from* this world, not the sort *this* world can produce. How can "thy kingdom come on earth," a kingdom where justice and love must reign, have nothing to do with this world and with politics? Jesus-Messiah, King of kings and Lord of lords.

Before Jesus ascended, he said that he would be with us until the end of this age—and that he will return! Let us see him now in each other, in others, in liturgy—especially in the reading of the gospel and in the Eucharist. And as for our glory, this morning's second reading says it well: "If you are insulted for the name of Christ, blessed are you, for the Spirit of Glory rests upon you."

Homily 21

JESUS, THE BRIDEGROOM: RETHINKING HEAVEN

WHEN PEOPLE COME TO me with various issues, I frequently ask them: If you had one wish, what would it be? What is your immense longing? When I tell them that they are ultimately seeking the kingdom of God, I often get a puzzled look. Still, our immense longing is for God, Christ, and a fully transformed creation, which is also called the new creation. This is *not* heaven in the popular sense! The all-too popular view that the meaning of life is to save our *souls* and go to *heaven* is definitely not Christianity. How common it is to think of heaven as non-material! This belief ignores that we are saved not as souls but as whole persons, resurrected *body-persons*, not in an ethereal heaven but as part of the new heaven and *the new earth*. This may surprise you, but the Scriptures say very little about going to heaven when we die. God's kingdom refers to God's sovereign rule coming on *earth* as it is in heaven. Biblical heaven is not a future destiny but the other, hidden dimension of ordinary life—God's transcendent dimension.

This morning's gospel portrays Jesus as the true Messiah, Israel's bridegroom, the fulfillment of Israel's deepest aspirations. The kingdom of God has arrived in person. Because Jesus is there, everything has changed for the better, so there is no room for fasting and mourning—although he points indirectly to the mourning that will follow when he is crucified.

Both in yesterday's and this morning's gospel, Jesus contradicts orthodox Jewish ways both of acting and their expectation of a messiah-king warrior who would overthrow the Roman occupiers, the pseudo-king

JESUS, THE BRIDEGROOM: RETHINKING HEAVEN

Herod, finish building the Temple, enforce strict observance of the Law, and restore Israel as a super-power. Even John the Baptist, whom many consider the highpoint of Jewish holiness is puzzled by Jesus' behavior and asked, "Are you he who is to come, or should we look for another?"

Jesus chose Matthew, a tax collector, a profession hated by the Jews. Matthew arose—a play on the word resurrection—and immediately followed Jesus. Jesus sat and ate with tax collectors and sinners to symbolize that the kingdom of God is open to everyone, not only to the so-called righteous who despised those with whom Jesus ate and associated. He and his disciples do not fast, which was the way observant Jews remembered the many tragedies in Israel history, especially the destruction of the Temple. Because of Jesus' presence, now is the time for feasting and rejoicing. The kingdom of God is here in person. In the words of Bobby Dillon, the sixties hippy, songwriter: "the times are a changin'."

Matthew's Gospel was written for the Jewish and gentile Christians in his community, and Jesus' teaching about the old and the new fits right in. Give up your old ways: Jesus crucified and risen has changed everything. He is Israel's true messiah, the savior of the entire world. The apostle Paul said that he considered everything he had lost as garbage in order to gain Christ. I have long pondered what he thought about when he was in prison awaiting possible death by the sword. He knew that in one sense the kingdom had not come: Herod was still king and the Romans still ruled. Yet Paul knew that the kingdom of God had arrived because the Father had raised Jesus from the dead. The times are a changin'.

Pope Francis's recent encyclical on the environment brings out the full meaning of Jesus as the seed of the kingdom in person. He wrote that the ultimate destiny of the entire universe is in the fullness of God, which has already been attained by the crucified and risen Christ. Does not the Book of Revelation teach that the Messiah-King-Lamb who sits with God on the throne makes *all things new* and that *every creature* in the new heaven and on the new earth and under the earth and in the sea, and all that is in them, shall praise and worship the slain lamb. Jesus, the Messiah-King, is not only the king of humans and angels, but also of animals, plants, insects, vegetation, rivers, oceans, the sun, the moon—the King also of the entire future new earth, here, where his creation is being fulfilled. That is our immense longing—not heaven in the popular sense. Is this your view of "heaven," with *all creation*, not only angels and humans? "The bridegroom is with them."

Homily 22

RETHINKING RESURRECTION AND HEAVEN AS THE NEW CREATION

"Christ has been raised from the dead."

TODAY'S FIRST READING FOCUSES on the heart and soul of Christianity: the bodily resurrection of the crucified Jesus-Messiah, the event on which the whole of human history turns. Christianity is a *resurrection* faith, a faith that loves God's good creation. Moreover, the New Testament defines *God* in a new way, as *the God and Father of our Lord Jesus Christ and the God who raised Jesus from the dead.*

Did Jesus die for our sins and rise for our justification? Of course! But he also died because *all creation groans* and Jesus was raised as *the seed of the new creation to usher in the new heaven and the new earth.* The *Boston Globe* writer, Alex Beam, caused quite a storm a few years ago when he claimed that dogs will be in heaven. I would go further. On the basis of my resurrection faith, I maintain that *all* animals, insects, vegetation, lakes, the stars, the moon, the oceans—all creation—will be part of the new heaven and the new earth depicted in the Book of Revelation. For this reason, popular views of heaven have to be rethought.

Who here has not had deep experiences of nature's beauty? Who here does not love wildlife? Close to me is a lovely reservoir, with its often breath-taking sunrises, sunsets, hawks, ducks, swans, and geese. I also find stirring some of the YouTube videos of humans interacting even with wild animals or various species of animals at play with each other.

RETHINKING RESURRECTION

My family always had a dog and I get great pleasure from the many dogs that walk the reservoir—especially "Bronx," the rescued pit bull and "Adonis," the golden retriever therapy dog. I've kissed a killer whale, nuzzled a domesticated Alaskan wolf, danced with an orangutan, surfed in the midst of porpoises, and seen a triple rainbow and the Aurora Borealis in Alaska. I fully expect to see again not only my mother and father, for example, but also God's *entire creation* resurrected and transformed, the new heaven and the new earth. God made us not only for himself, not only for each other, but also for his entire creation. This is unfortunately not the popular view of heaven.

The Book of Genesis tells us that God not only created everything good but also that God established a rainbow covenant with Noah, his descendants, and every living creature on earth. The prophet Hosea also underscores God's rainbow covenant with all creation and the prophet Isaiah writes of creation's full restoration. Jesus is also specific when he proclaimed that his Father does not forget even the lowly sparrow. What was, is, and will be—all creation—will exist forever—resurrected, transformed. In addition, when the Jewish Scriptures speak of a fast being proclaimed, the domesticated animals are included. The sounds of distress from fasting animals must have added to the penitential atmosphere.

John's Gospel and the apostle Paul emphasize that through Christ all things have been created, in him all things hold together—and that Christ is all, and in all. Read Teilhard de Chardin's compelling view of the cosmic Christ in his masterpiece, *The Divine Milieu*. The Book of Revelation speaks of the Lamb on the throne making all things new and of every creature in the new heaven and on the new earth and under the earth and in the sea, and all that is in them, singing a hymn of praise to the slain lamb. Ignatius of Loyola would have us ponder how not only the saints intercede and pray for us but also "the heavens, the sun, the moon, the stars, the elements, the fruits, the birds, fish, and animals." His "Contemplation to Obtain Divine Love" also focuses on all creation as a theophany. And how he loved to contemplate the stars. Rejoicing in creation as a theophany is, of course, as old as the Psalms. St. Francis of Assisi's "Canticle of Brother Sun" is another paean to the interconnection of all creation as a single theophany.

One of my favorite, however, is penned by the fourteenth-century Dominican mystic Henry Suso who complains that his sins keep him from praising God. "Dear Lord," he writes, "the frogs in the ditches praise you. And if they can't sing, at least they croak." God assures him that "there was never a creature so small or so great, so good or so bad, nor will there ever be one, that did not praise or show that I am worthy of praise." So, let us at least croak for God! And because Christ has been raised from the dead, this will be also be true in the new heaven and the new earth.

Homily 23

FEAST OF CHRIST THE KING

"Jesus, King of kings and Lord of lords"

When the prophet Samuel was getting old, the Israelite elders demanded a king in order to be like other nations. When Samuel prayed, the Lord God said: "Listen! They have rejected me as their king. . . . Warn them that a king will take for his own use a good portion of their sons and daughters, livestock, fields, vineyards, and grain and—they will become his slaves." Still, the people refused to listen to Samuel and cried out: "No! We want a king over us." Then the Lord God said to the prophet: "All right, give them a king."

"How about Donald Trump," Samuel asked? "No," the Lord God said, "He wants my job." "Valdimir Putin?," asked Samuel. "No," the Lord God said, "He's already causing trouble in Ukraine and elsewhere." "Select Saul." "But he is a nutcase," Samuel objected. "Yes, I know," the Lord God said, "but he will unite my chosen people and indirectly pave the way for David, his son-in-law, who will not only be a great king, but also the one from whose seed will come the true Messiah-King not only of Israel but also of the entire world."

Then the Lord God asked: "Samuel, you have the new Apple iPad pro, what do you foresee?" The prophet replied: "King David will be an adulterer and a murderer, but he will repent and beget the great king Solomon who will build your Temple. But after that, I see a long line of disastrous, evil kings who will even end David's line. For example, although not of

David's seed, Herod will be rewarded with kingship by the Romans because of his military victories."

"Well done, prophet," the Lord God said: "Now I'll tell you the rest of the story. I shall place a great star in the sky for the Magi from the east to follow. They will then be told by Jewish authorities that the true Messiah-King of David's seed, can be found in David's town, Bethlehem. There the Magi will worship him."

But then the prophet's iPad rebooted and Samuel prophesied further: "Herod, however, will try to kill Jesus, the Messiah-King, by massacring all baby boys under two." The Lord God said: "He will not succeed and my faithful servant Simeon will recognize Jesus as the consolation of Israel when he is circumcised. He will grow up in Nazareth, leave, and be baptized in the Jordan as the new Moses by John of the Baptist, 'this is my beloved son, listen to him.' He will preach that the kingdom of God will be ushered in through his person and his mighty deeds. This Messiah-King will gather disciples—who will not understand what my true Messiah-King and kingdom really are, a kingdom not *from* the world but very much for the world. And he will make many enemies. He will be arrested and handed over to Roman soldiers who will place on him a purple robe and a crown of thorns, spit on and strike him, and mocking fall on their knees crying out, 'Hail, king of the Jews.'"

"How come you know so much about the Scriptures, Lord God," asked Samuel? "Well, I wrote them," the Lord God said. "Furthermore, Pilate will question Jesus about his kingship and ridicule him when Jesus speaks of truth, not knowing that when theologians criticized my servant Job for questioning my ways, my beloved Thomas Aquinas said: 'Job spoke the truth and I, God, am Truth.' Is it not ironic that Jesus-Messiah is the way, *the truth*, and the life, and Pilate does not even recognize truth when my enfleshed Truth stands before him?"

Furthermore, "Is it not the supreme irony that when Pilate asked the Jewish authorities, 'Shall I crucify your king?,' that they replied, 'we have no king but Caesar,'—a despot they hated? Also, did not the solders and the high priests ridicule Jesus on the cross and say: 'If he is the king of Israel; let him now come down from the cross, and we will believe in him.' Is not the sign on the cross *INRI*, Latin for 'Jesus of Nazareth, king of the Jews?'"

Confused, the prophet Samuel asked the Lord God: "How come you know Latin and so much else but I am only a prophet?" "Well," God replied: "you made the mistake of going to Harvard for a degree in prophecy. I went to Boston College for a degree in Arts and Sciences and then a doctorate in theology. So, I know everything—but that is all I know."

"One more thing, Samuel. Pope Francis's recent encyclical on the environment brings out the full meaning of today's Solemnity of Christ the King. He wrote that the ultimate destiny of the entire universe is in the fullness of God, which has already been attained by the risen Christ. Did not the apostle Paul write that in Jesus all things have been created, in him all things hold together—and that because of Jesus I shall be all and in all and Jesus, too? Does not the Book of Revelation teach that the Messiah-King-Lamb who sits with me on the throne makes all things new and that every creature in the new heaven and on the new earth and under the earth and in the sea, and all that is in them, shall praise and worship the slain lamb. Jesus, the Messiah-King, is not only the King of humans and angels, but also of animals, insects, vegetation, rivers, oceans, the sun, the moon—the King also of the entire future new earth and the new heaven. "Jesus, King of kings and Lord of lords."

Homily 24

PENTECOST SUNDAY

"Receive the Holy Spirit."

I WOULD CALL TODAY's feast of Pentecost the bubbling enthusiasm of Jesus' disciples for finally realizing what it means to be a Christian. Bubbling enthusiasm: when I was a boy, I woke up early one Christmas morning, raced down the stairs, and there it was: an electric train set. My bubbling enthusiasm caused me to rush to wake my sister. Our parents were at Mass, returned home to find us playing with our gifts, but disappointed at not being there to see our bubbling enthusiasm when we first saw our gifts.

Whenever I do a wedding, the bubbling enthusiasm on the bride's face always impresses me. The look of bubbling enthusiasm when a mother and father gaze upon their newborn, a look I often see when I baptize. My parents and sister remarked about my bubbling enthusiasm when I was ordained and then saying my First Mass.

I have old friends, husband and wife, who made a charismatic retreat years ago. For weeks afterwards, she would cry out with bubbling enthusiasm: "I am a Christian, I am a Christian." Her husband wanted to strangle her. If you have ever been to a charismatic meeting or spoken with one touched with the bubbling enthusiasm of those in the charismatic movement, you have an idea of what Jesus' disciples experienced on Pentecost and how they acted—for a while.

In this morning's gospel, the risen Christ appears to his disciples and announces: "Receive the Holy Spirit." But during another resurrection appearance, Jesus ordered his disciples not to leave Jerusalem because there

PENTECOST SUNDAY

they would later be baptized with the Holy Spirit, receive power, and become his witnesses. So they went to Jerusalem during the Jewish feast of Pentecost, a pilgrim feast, the last feast of Passover, the Jewish harvest festival, which also commemorates the giving of the Law to Moses on Mount Sinai.

Because resurrection was associated with the age to come, Jesus' disciples probably expected the end of this existing age. But what happened to them? They "were all filled with the Holy Spirit," Jesus' Spirit—the Christian experience. Tongues as of fire transformed them from confused, fearful disciples to those who would courageously, publicly preach—as if drunk with new wine, with bubbling enthusiasm—in different languages to the entire world (thus the list of known areas of the world)—the Good News of the Lord Jesus-Messiah—and—in the face of the full hostile force of Jewish and Roman authority.

Unfortunately, bubbling enthusiasm does not last. Jesus himself must have been bored at times— his disciples failure to understand and listening to their bickering about who is the greatest in the kingdom of God. Even in good, stable marriages, humdrum daily life takes over. And how many married couples resonate with this? A wife became so angry with her husband that she told him to get out and yelled as he went through the door: "I hope you die a long, slow, painful death." He turned around and said, "So, you want me to stay?"

At my grandnephew's confirmation, I was struck forcefully by the boredom of one priest—a very good and loved priest—who had just celebrated his fifteenth anniversary. I had a nun friend who said there were times when she said that she wished she has said yes to George's proposal years ago! Humdrum, daily life takes a toll. The great German Jesuit theologian, Karl Rahner, confessed on his 80th birthday that he was not exactly bursting with joy!

Although faithful to Jesus to the end, the apostles eventually had to deal with the ins and outs of daily living with the sober intoxication of the Spirit, especially with people who ignored or laughed at their message, the beatings, imprisonment, and in some cases, the death they received from both Jewish and Roman authorities. What sustained the apostle Paul in prison—awaiting death by the sword (no crucifixion for a Roman citizen)? Herod was still king, the Romans still controlled Israel, and the Temple was still not completed. Paul's sober intoxication: "I want only to know Christ and him crucified."

What sustained Pope John Paul II during his long period of physical decline or Cardinal Avery Dulles whose polio reawakened in later life, confining him to a wheel chair, and rendered him almost speechless? Persevering through the grayness of everyday life in faith, hope, and love by carrying the cross of our often humdrum, daily lives is the more sober form of Pentecost. We should also keep in mind the first Pentecost: Christ on the *cross* giving up his spirit. The Spirit is born in blood. The apostle Paul was less interested in Pentecostal bubbling enthusiasm and more with the fruits of the Spirit: love, joy, peace, forbearance, kindness, goodness, faithfulness, gentleness and self-control. There is no law against these, he wrote.

With this in mind, let us pray to do the ordinary in an extraordinary way—filled with the courage and hope we have from the Pentecostal Spirit of the crucified and risen Jesus-Messiah. "Receive the Holy Spirit."

Homily 25

TRINITY SUNDAY

"Glory be to the Father, to the Son, and to the Holy Spirit."

POPE FRANCIS CLAIMED THAT homilies are a torture both for those preparing and those hearing them. If you listened carefully last evening, then you heard the screams of priests trying to write a homily on Christianity's greatest mystery, the Trinity. Listen carefully now and you will catch the shrieks or snores of those in parishes—not here, though—hearing about the mystery that the Father is God; the Son is God; the Holy Spirit is God, but that the Father is not the Son or the Holy Spirit. The mystery of the one God but three persons.

When studying in Germany, I overheard in a train station two businessmen discussing the Trinity. They asserted that [expletive deleted] Catholic priests imported the doctrine from Egypt. I objected, but before I could explain, I was simply told off: "Get lost, foreigner." I gave a lecture on the Trinity years ago to a group of contemplative men. Before the talk, some told me they were attending only because their superior had commanded them under obedience. They said that the Trinity was a pure theological abstraction that certainly had nothing—so they thought—with their Christian and prayer life. Some way to begin a talk.

When I entered the Jesuits, St. Ignatius of Loyola's profound trinitarian mysticism fascinated me. He prayed—not to God in general—but to the Father *as* Father, to the Son as Son, and to the Holy Spirit as Holy Spirit—and whom he *experienced* as such. Do you and I experience the Trinity that dwells within us? My love of the Trinity received the frosting on the cake because my Mass the day after my ordination was Trinity Sunday. So, today, is in some ways my anniversary.

When God created Adam, he said that it was not good for man to be alone and created Eve. The two became one flesh. Marriage: a symbol of how two can be truly one. The aging doctor in the lovely novel, *Corelli's Mandolin*, tells his daughter that he and her mother started out as two trees who had become one and how her birth had make them a family, three in one. A pale reflection of the eternal Trinity.

Unlike human families with their sometimes frictions and conflicts, however, the triune God dwells in perfect self-communicating truth and love. Some medieval mystics wrote of the eternal dance of truth and love of the Father, the Son, and the Holy Spirit. God as three-in-one means that not even God is alone. And *we* shall dance eternally with the Trinity. My dance card is already filled out for flamenco with the Holy Spirit.

The fourteenth-century Dominican mystic-theologian, Meister Eckhart, wrote: "When God laughs at the soul and the soul laughs back at God, the persons of the Trinity are begotten. When the Father laughs at the Son and the Son laughs back at the Father, that laugh gives pleasure, that pleasure gives joy, that joy gives love, and that love is the Holy Spirit." Unorthodox, but still lovely.

When Jesus was baptized in the Jordan, the Holy Spirit descended upon him and the Father said: "This is my beloved Son, listen to him." The Trinity! Jesus commanded his disciples to go forth and to baptize in the name of the Father, the Son, and the Holy Spirit. Notice, he said "name," not "names," which underscores the *one* God in three persons. I know many persons who are deeply consciousness of the Trinity living within them. What a great gift. How conscious are you of this reality?

I suggest, therefore, that you pray to the Father as Father, God-above-us, the ever-greater God, holy Mystery, the divine Abyss wild and deep who corresponds to our immense longing to worship, to surrender to the blessed, incomprehensible Father's enfleshed Word, Light, and Truth in history. He who sees me sees the Father! Jesus, the Father's promised yes to us. We are an immense longing to find the one person in history, this earth, our life, who will totally fulfill us. This is found in the incarnate, crucified, and resurrected Jesus Christ. The Holy Spirit is the love the Father and the Son poured into our hearts, God-in-us, the embrace and kiss of the Father and Son who embraces and kisses our souls, who draws us into our deepest

TRINITY SUNDAY

selves. Often frightened of our deepest self, we still desire to be plunged into the abyss we are because the Spirit of love dwells there.

Father, Son, and Holy Spirit, as God-above, -with, and -in us, God as Mystery, Truth, and Love. The one God, God-above-us, who always remains mystery, has given himself to be God-with-us and God-in-us, love itself. Please allow me close with St.. Ignatius of Loyola's instructions: "When we make the holy sign of the cross, we place our fingers first on the head; and this is to signify God our Father, who proceeds from no one. (There is one God because there is one Father.) When we touch our breast, this signifies the Son, our Lord, who proceeds from the Father and who descended into the womb of the blessed Virgin Mary. When we place our fingers on both shoulders, this signifies the Holy Spirit, who proceeds from the Father and the Son. And when we fold our hands together again, this symbolizes that the three persons are one single God. And finally, when we seal our lips with the sign of the cross, this means that in Jesus, our savior and redeemer, dwells the Father, the Son, and Holy Spirit, one single God, our creator and Lord—and that the divinity was never separated from the body of Jesus, not even at his death." Glory be to the Father and to the Son and to the Holy Spirit."

HOMILIES CENTERED ON JESUS CHRIST

Homily 26

WHO DO YOU SAY THAT I AM?

"Blessed are you, Simon son of Jonah, for this was not revealed to you by flesh and blood, but by my Father in heaven.

IT IS STRIKING THAT when Peter identifies Jesus as the Christ, God's Messiah, Jesus rebukes both him and the disciples and gives them strict orders not to say this to anyone. Why does Jesus prohibit this? Many Jews of Jesus' day were expecting a warrior-king-messiah who would defeat the Roman occupiers, depose the pseudo-king Herod, complete the construction of the Temple, ensure that all Jews kept the Law, and reestablish Israel as a superpower. A suffering, crucified messiah made no sense.

Thus Jesus announces his coming passion, death, and resurrection and that a true disciple must bear the cross daily. What a reversal of expectations! This is certainly a rejoinder to Freud's nonsense that Christianity is the projection of human dreams and wishes. Do you wish to be crucified daily? How would you answer Jesus' question, "Who do *you* say that I am?"

When I taught at Santa Clara University many years ago, I befriended a young Buddhist priest, pastor of a Buddhist parish in Los Gatos. He told me that curious Christians often visited and asked what he thought about Christianity. He told them that Christianity's foundation is the person of Jesus Christ who is confessed and worshipped as the crucified and risen God-man by people who are the mystical body of Christ. My Buddhist friend would have answered Jesus correctly. Do you resonate with that reply?

I would also reply to Jesus: "You could be displeasing, incomprehensible, radical. You actually said that unless a person hates mother and father one cannot be your disciple; cut off your foot, pluck out your eye, if they lead you to sin; you said to parents, as evil as you are, you know how to give good things to your children; you addressed those listening to you as belonging to an evil generation; you said to leave the dead to bury the dead. (A primary duty of children was to bury parents and others.)

Who do you say that I am? To which I would also reply: "Jesus, your mercy and gentleness with sinners stands out. You are God the Father's merciful, forgiving, and healing love in the flesh. You asked the adulterous woman about to be stoned, "Has anyone condemned you? Neither do I. Do not sin again." You said to the Samaritan woman at the well, "and the one you are living with now is not your husband," but you allowed her to change the subject. You commanded us to forgive seventy-times-seven times, a Jewish way of saying every time; when you appeared to your disciples after the resurrection, you never chastised them for their cowardly abandonment but bestowed your messianic peace upon them.

Who do you say that I am? During an ecumenical seminar of high-powered theologians in Germany, Karl Rahner, the famous twentieth-century theologian, startled many of the participants and his audience when he said: "You really cannot answer that question unless, like the Beloved Disciple, you have quickly recognized him as Lord, and like Peter, plunged into the sea of life to reach him, fallen in love with him, and thrown your arms around him as your crucified and risen savior." I suggest that we should do that especially when we receive him during communion.

Moreover, "who do you say that I am?" You, Jesus, are everyone in need—be it spiritual or physical—as Mother Teresa knew so well.

Homily 27

JESUS: CHRISTIANITY'S HEART

"His own received him not."

THIS MORNING'S FIRST READING continues what followed from the disciples' preaching of Jesus' mighty deeds and of his death, resurrection, ascension, glorification, and his giving of the Holy Spirit. Although many of Jesus' own people became Christians, the apostle Paul wrote of a "mysterious hardening" that came upon them, and, as St. John wrote, "his own received him not."

One of the great blessings in my life was to become deeply aware that Jesus was a first-century Judean Jew and that the first Christians were Jews. Ignatius of Loyola wished that he were Jewish, to be related to Jesus by blood. Pope Pius XI said that we Christians are spiritual Semites and that one cannot hate the Jews and be a Christian. Both for St. Paul and St. Luke in Acts of the Apostles, this "hardening" of Jesus' own people was a great blessing for the gentiles who were delighted and glorified the word of God. Acts of the Apostles proclaims, "the number of disciples increased greatly. Even a large group of priests became believers." How quickly the power of the gospel and the mysterious "hardening" that came over Israel transformed Jesus' followers from a Jewish sect to a world-wide church. I have said Mass in Asia, Africa, North and South America, Europe, and Australia—never in Antarctica, because the penguins remain resolute pagans.

Jesus' own people came to reject him not only because he put human welfare above the Sabbath, declared all foods clean, and predicted the destruction of the Temple but also because he made himself God's equal.

No Jew, no Buddha, no wise man of India, would have ever dared to say, "whoever has seen me has seen the Father," or the Father and I are one." Jesus has been called the sacrament of the encounter with God the Father. He has been called *the human face of God*. The Jews and even Moses feared to look upon God's face. But as St. Paul wrote, "we now have the light of the knowledge of the glory of God in the *face* of Christ" and are able to gaze upon the human face of God and live.

This morning, let us become more aware that we are, a "royal priesthood," a people who worship a Jew. Let us become more aware, too, how frequently the New Testament speaks not simply of "God" but of the "God and Father of our Lord Jesus Christ" and of "the God who raised Jesus from the dead." The God of the Old Testament is now defined by his relationship to the crucified and risen Jesus. Christianity is an Easter faith that sees everything in the light of Jesus crucified and risen. Given the confusion about Christianity in our times, I always ask those with whom I speak: what is Christianity? It is the worship of the person of the triune crucified and risen Christ and those who profess him as Lord and who pray through his Holy Spirit: "Abba, Father."

Homily 28

JESUS' CENTRAL MESSAGE: THE KINGDOM

"Thy kingdom come on earth as it is in heaven."

ONE OF THE GREAT blessings of my priestly and theological life was the rediscovery by scholars that Jesus must be understood as a first-century, second Temple, Judean Jew whose central message focused on the kingdom of God—not universal love, as one often hears. The famous scholar, N. T. Wright, has an appendix in one of his many books that lists the astonishing number of references to the kingdom of God in the Scriptures. The Jewish longing during Jesus' day was for the arrival of God's kingdom, for God to be faithful to his covenant promises, forgive them, free them the oppression of their Roman occupiers, overthrow the pseudo-king Herod, have all Jews perfectly observe the Law, complete the building of the Temple, thus fulfilling the covenant promises that God was their God and they were God's people. I cannot overemphasize that the Jewish understanding—and thus Jesus' understanding of the kingdom of God—was very much a kingdom *of this world*, with strong political overtones.

This view is the context for understanding the phrase, "thy kingdom come on earth," in the Our Father prayer. Jesus' person, mission, and preaching stressed that the kingdom of God was breaking in because *Jesus* was present. His person, his exorcisms, his raising of the dead, his many parables, and his miracles all stressed that Israel's history had reached its climactic moment, that Israel's dream was coming true right then and there. In short, Jesus is the kingdom incarnate, the seed of what will fully flower in

Israel fulfilled and the world transformed into thy kingdom come *on earth as it is in heaven*. Jesus *never* said my kingdom is not of this world. This is a bad translation. It should be, my kingdom is not *from* this world, not the sort that comes from this world. Jesus never said that the kingdom of God is *within you*—again, an infelicitous translation—but the kingdom of God is in your midst—I am here—or the kingdom of God is within your grasp.

When the apostle Paul was in prison, he knew that in one sense the kingdom had not come: Herod was still king and the Romans nonetheless ruled. Yet Paul knew that Jesus was in fact the breaking in of the kingdom because the Father had raised him from the dead. Because of Jesus' resurrection, Paul and we know that God is indeed among his people, God-with-us, Emmanuel, unconditional love incarnate. In the risen Christ, as the seed of the kingdom of God, all creation, which groans, is being brought to perfect fulfillment and transformation—you, I, the entire creation will be raised from the dead as the new heavens and the new earth. That is the kingdom of God. "Thy kingdom come *on earth* as it is in heaven!"

Homily 29

JESUS THE JEW AND THE FEAST OF THE IMMACULATE HEART OF MARY

"Each year Jesus' parents went to Jerusalem for the feast of Passover"

THIS MORNING'S GOSPEL FOCUSES on the twelve-year old Jesus going up to Jerusalem to celebrate the Jewish feast of Passover with his parents, relatives, and acquaintances. Jesus, a first-century, Second-Temple Jew, took part in the same observances and celebrations as his people. When my mother's acerbic neighbor scoffed at our family Christmas celebration, saying, "we Jehovah's Witnesses celebrate nothing," I calmly said, "then you are neither Christian nor even human."

Jesus not only celebrated the Jewish religious feasts but he also rejoiced with his people at weddings, at Cana, for example, changing roughly one-hundred-eighty gallons of water into wine. How often in the gospels do we find Jesus at feasts, meals, and eating with his disciples and others! It is not surprising that the key image of the kingdom of God is the messianic banquet. Jesus was no desert ascetic, such as John the Baptist. The Jewish people knew how to celebrate, rejoice, dance, sing, eat good food, and drink good wine—as they do to this day. And Jesus was no exception. How he loved to sing and dance at wedding, and to eat the Thanksgiving turkey and the Fourth of July lobsters and steamers!

The late Henry Ford, the founder of the Ford motor company, had such a hatred of Jews that he wrote a book arguing that Jesus was not a Jew.

HOMILIES IN A NEW KEY

Many Enlightenment scholars also attempted to dissociate Jesus from his Jewish roots. Jesus Christ, with Christ as a proper name, is another way of obscuring Jesus' radical Jewish identity. He is Jesus-Messiah, the long-promised *anointed one* of Israel. As we read in John's Gospel, "The first thing Andrew did was to find his brother Simon and tell him, 'We have found the Messiah' (that is, the Christ)."

During a dinner at which some guests denigrated the Jews, St. Ignatius of Loyola shocked them when he said that he wished he were Jewish in order to be related to Jesus by blood. Ignatius also had a great desire to live and work in the Holy Land in order to walk in Jesus' footsteps. One of the great blessings in my life came from those scholars who show without a doubt that Jesus was a first-century, Second-Temple Judean Jew who saw himself as the consolation of Israel, *the* Messiah foretold by the prophets, as the one who would bring Israel's history as God's chosen people to be the light of the world to its victorious conclusion. Jesus not only said, " I am the light of the world," but also, "salvation is from the Jews."

The apostle Paul proclaimed: "For I am not ashamed of the gospel, because it is the power of God that brings salvation to everyone who believes: first to the Jew, then to the Gentile" and wrote of Jesus-Messiah as the power and wisdom of God. Notice, *first to the Jew*, then to the gentile. Furthermore, "there is neither Jew nor Gentile, neither slave nor free, nor is there male and female, for you are all one in Christ Jesus. If you belong to Christ, then you are Abraham's seed, and heirs according to the promise." In short, whoever is in Jesus-Messiah is of Abraham's seed. Who is the true Jew? The one with a circumcised heart.

In the apostle Paul's famous Epistle to the Romans, he writes; "Has God rejected his people? By no means! Of those of my own race, the people of Israel: theirs is the adoption as sons; theirs the divine glory, the covenants, the receiving of the law, the Temple worship and the promises. Theirs are the patriarchs, and from them is traced the human ancestry of Christ, who is God over all, forever praised! Amen." If you read the letters of the apostle Paul properly, you will notice how Paul stresses that Jesus-Messiah is the *transformation and fulfillment* of Israel's entire history, especially of the promises God made to Abraham: "you are my chosen people." And Christians are of Abraham's seed.

As early as 1938, Pope Pius XI wrote that Christians are spiritual Semites. Pope St. John Paul II, who made headlines in 1986 as the first pope to visit Rome's main synagogue and declared Jews to be the "elder brothers" of

THE FEAST OF THE IMMACULATE HEART OF MARY

the Christian faith. Recently Pope Francis said that inside every Christian is a Jew. Christianity is not another religion but Judaism perfected.

This morning's gospel also focuses on Mary keeping all things about Jesus in her heart. Let us do the same. At the wedding feast in Cana we hear Mary's last recorded words: "Listen to him." Let us also do that.

Homily 30

JESUS' AUTHORITY

"They glorified God who had given such authority to men!"

WHEN I READ THIS morning's gospel, I thought of an American Jesuit at our university in Seoul, Korea who was puzzled that American Catholic students do not respect the authority of the pope and their bishops. I told him that this ignoring of official authority was not only true of American students but also of adults here and many countries where Catholics shrug their shoulders when papal or episcopal authority is mentioned.

Most contemporary American that I have dealt with, however, respect *personal* authority—in the same way that people were awed by Jesus' authority that was unlike that that of the Scribes and Pharisees. I remember a diminutive nun who taught at Santa Clara University scolding a huge football player for his drunken behavior the night before—and his childlike behavior with her. Many non-Catholics—and even some quite anti-Catholic people—never missed a broadcast of Monsignor Fulton Sheen because he spoke to their hearts. Pope Francis seems to have this charism. I know several Jesuits here at Boston College who have more authority with students than the local bishops.

My Connecticut niece's husband needs only one look at his children or the dog misbehaving in order for their behavior to change. Authority. My orthopedic surgeon told me of a Jesuit who took over a classroom midsemester at Boston College High when the former teacher was fired for incompetence. He said that the students shuddered when this Jesuit came

JESUS' AUTHORITY

into the classroom, recognized his personal authority, and later said that he was one of the best teachers they had ever had.

Neither Pilate nor Herod nor the Pharisees nor the Scribes possessed the authority Jesus had. Jesus had authority in this teaching, over diseases—even at a distance—over demons, and over storms. The disciples were terrified and asked each other, "Who is this? Even the wind and the waves obey him!" He even forgave sins. "Who can forgive sins except God alone?"

The Jews of Jesus' day believed that physical paralysis came upon a person because of certain kinds of sin. Notice that Jesus called attention to the faith of the paralytic sinner and his friends. He forgave the paralytic his sins and the official authorities went wild: "Who can forgive sins except God alone?" Then Jesus upped the ante. That they may know that the Son of Man has God's authority, he told the paralytic to arise—and he did. When sin is forgiven, *resurrection* is not far off. And the crowds were struck with awe.

I spent two months in a wheel chair after an accident. To the annoyance of the nurse and superiors, I would cross campus in my wheel chair, travel down Beacon street, then come up Commonwealth Avenue—about a half-mile trip. I would frequently meet the most awkward jogger that I had ever seen. When I started walking, I met him and he shouted with joy, awe, and put his two thumbs up. Awe at a minor resurrection!

Pope Francis recently spoke about his bedtime prayer, "Lord Jesus, make me clean," which he recited five times, each with an our Father, and one for each of Jesus' glorious wounds through which we are healed. What paralyzes you in great or small ways? Use Francis's prayer, but change it. "Lord, free me from what paralyzes me." Repeat it five times and place each in Jesus' glorious wounds. "They glorified God who had given such authority to men!"

Homily 31

HE WHO SEES ME SEES THE FATHER

"I and the Father are one."

THIS MORNING SECOND READING focuses on the apostle Paul's magnificent hymn to Jesus in whom all things hold together. John's Gospel echoes this hymn when Jesus says, "he who sees me sees the Father."

Shortly before his death, the atheist, Christopher Hitchens, spoke of Jesus Christ as a madman and megalomaniac. I liked what the atheist Hitchens said because he read the New Testament correctly. Either Jesus is who he said he is or he is a madman. For example, Jesus' disciples undoubtedly followed him because they thought he was a prophet, a teacher, or even the promised Messiah—but Jesus kept raising the stakes. What prophet would have dared to forgive sins, to place his law above what God had commanded through Moses concerning murder, retaliation, adultery, and the like? Jesus proclaimed: "God said through Moses, but I say to you!" Besides, what prophet would have claimed to be greater than the Temple, Solomon, and Jonah? What prophet would have claimed that he and the Father are one, that only he had seen the Father, that he who sees him sees the Father, who addressed himself as "I AM," the name God revealed to Moses, and that salvation comes only through him? An incredible historical fact: his disciples, Jews, eventually worshipped this human being as my Lord and my God.

My niece's family has a very bright beagle-basset mix dog, "Hazel." Supposing one day she began to speak, to read and write, to discuss politics. One would ask: What do have we here? The disciples' awareness grew that

HE WHO SEES ME SEES THE FATHER

they were following more than a mere man—Jesus, the image of the invisible God. My Lord and my God!

When I taught at Santa Clara University in the early seventies, I befriended a young Buddhist priest, pastor of a Buddhist parish in Los Gatos. He related to me that curious Christians often visited and asked him what he thought about Christianity. He told them that Christianity's foundation is the *person* of Jesus Christ who is confessed and *worshipped* as the crucified and *risen* God-man. The Buddhist pastor was spot on. What would you have said Christianity is all about?

In a conversation with a Jehovah's Witness, he told me that Jesus was not God because he prayed. Of course the God-*MAN* prayed. In addition to what I just said, I told him to read Cardinal Pierre de Bérulle, a seventeenth–eighteenth century French mystic, who wrote: "And just as there is a God worthy of being adored, served and loved, so there is also in you, O Jesus my Lord, a God adoring, loving and serving him eternally without any defect in this adoration, and a God who adores, without detracting from his divinity!" *A God adored and a God adoring.*

During an ecumenical seminar in Germany, the German Jesuit theologian, Karl Rahner, startled many of the participants when he said: "You really cannot do Christology unless you have fallen in love with Jesus, thrown your arms around him, and confess with Thomas, " my Lord and my God." Likewise, when asked what was the most important contemporary theological problem, Rahner responded: "How can I truly experience that in *Jesus Christ God* has communicated himself to us in an *absolute and irreversible way*?

Pope Francis's recent encyclical on the environment proclaims that the ultimate destiny of the entire universe is in the fullness of God, which has already been attained by the *crucified and risen Jesus-Messiah*, through whom and for whom all things were created. Francis called attention to the Book of Revelation, which teaches that the Messiah-King-Lamb who sits with God on the throne makes *all things new* and that *every creature* in the new heaven and on the new earth and under the earth and in the sea, and all that is in them, shall praise and worship the slain lamb. Notice: *every* creature, not only humans and angels.

Not many years ago, I kissed a killer whale. Despite the name "killer," these mammals are highly intelligent and like human beings. I also danced with an wild orangutan, surfed with playful dolphins, snorkeled in the midst of black tipped sharks, nuzzled a domesticated Alaskan wolf, and patted a former fighting pit bull, named Bronx—no ears and rescued by the young man with whom I spoke. Will all these lovely creatures be in the new creation? Definitely!

My view of the new creation is consonant with what Pope Francis wrote: "Jesus, the Messiah-King, is not only the king of humans and angels, but also of animals, fish, insects, vegetation, rivers, oceans, the stars, the sun, the moon—the king of the entire future new earth, here, where his creation is being fulfilled." That is our immense longing—not *heaven* in the popular sense. We all want God, Christ, a fully transformed self, *and* a fully transformed creation that God deemed good. "Christ Jesus is the image of the invisible God."

Homily 32

THE OFFENSIVE JESUS

"And they took offense at him."

I ASK YOU NOW the same question Jesus asked his disciples: Who do you say that Jesus is? What is your image of Jesus? An astonishing number of people have a romantic view of Jesus that in no way correlates with the gospel Jesus. He is often wrongly depicted as gentle Jesus, meek, mild—nice, who wants us all to be nice to each other, happy, and to feel good about ourselves. This "nice" Jesus teaches that God loves everyone exactly as they are, that they need not change anything in their lives, as long as they try to be good to others, and that one religion is as good as another.

The actual Jesus, however, is a first-century, Second-Temple Judean Jew who claims that he, in his person, is actually ushering in God's kingdom *on earth*. This kingdom of love, justice, truth, mercy, and holiness makes *tremendous* demands on those committed to Jesus' agenda. For example, what does one make of a so-called agreeable Jesus who says: "If anyone does not hate father and mother, wife, children, brothers, sisters—even his or her own life—cannot be my disciple?" How does one assess a supposedly sweet Jesus who proclaims that he had come to turn a son against his father, a daughter against her mother, a daughter-in-law against her mother-in-law, and that one's enemies will be those of one's own household? How could a so-called *nice* Jesus declare: " I have come *not* to bring peace but a sword?" Why does this sweet Jesus insist that you will be *hated* by everyone because of him and that you are *blessed* when people insult you, persecute you, and falsely say all kinds of evil things against you—because of him? What sort of *nice* Jesus would urge you cut off and throw away any part of your body that causes you to sin—otherwise your whole body will be thrown into hell? How many of us would have any body parts left? This supposedly nice Jesus demands that we love our enemies, turn the other cheek, forgive seventy-times-seven times, carry our cross daily, and be willing even to give up our own life for another.

Jesus shocked not only the Jewish hierarchy but also observant Jews when he declared all foods clean (the Maccabean martyrs chose death rather than eat unclean food), that he was Lord of the Sabbath, and that the Temple was doomed. Try cooking meat for a vegan, pork for a Muslim, or convincing a fundamentalist that it is all right to play golf on Sunday.

It is obvious that this supposedly sweet Jesus also said rather harsh things to people. He called some hypocrites, fools, blind guides, whitewashed tombs, serpents, a brood of vipers, lawless, liars, those without understanding, and children of Satan. He warned his disciples not to give to dogs (a racial slur for pagans) what is sacred or to throw their pearls to swine, the animal considered the most unclean by Jews. Even his own duh-ciples (*sic*) were not spared: "Are you also without understanding? Are you dense?" He chided them on more than one occasion and even called the great apostle Peter a "Satan." Consider the ordinary people in his audience, whom he called an "evil generation" and told them, "as evil as you are, you know how to give good things to your children." A *nice* Jesus?

This supposedly *nice* universal Jesus insisted that salvation *comes from the Jews*. When a Canaanite woman, a pagan, came to him and began to cry out, "have mercy on me, Lord, son of David; my daughter is cruelly demon-possessed," Jesus ignored her and remained silent. His disciples begged him to send her away. But Jesus said, "I was sent *only* to the lost sheep of the *house of Israel*." Then he said to the pagan woman, "It is not good to take the children's bread, that of the Jews, and throw it to the dogs" (that is, the pagans).

Consonant with Jesus' insistence that his mission was to the Jews (although he did cure the Canaanite woman's daughter and the Roman centurion's servant), the apostle Paul stressed that God had not abandoned his chosen people. He insisted: "*Theirs* is the adoption to sonship; *theirs* the divine glory, the covenants, the receiving of the Law, the Temple worship, and the promises. *Theirs* are the patriarchs, and from them is traced the human ancestry of Jesus-Messiah, who is God over all, forever praised!" The apostle to the gentiles also stressed: "*First for the Jew*, then for the gentile."

THE OFFENSIVE JESUS

Why did the apostle Peter proclaim that salvation is found in no other name, Jesus' name? No religious indifference exists there either.

Jesus' words and actions were so outrageous that some of his relatives and the town's people did not believe in him. Along with the Jewish authorities, many said that he was out of his mind, possessed by Beelzebul, a drunkard, a glutton, a bastard, a Samaritan (a racial slur as provocative as the "n" word in our culture.), and one who leads the people astray—thus a false prophet deserving of the harshest punishment. This so-called *nice* Jesus so infuriated the people of Nazareth that they seized him, thrust him out of the city, and led him to the brow of the hill that they might cast him down headlong. And when Jesus declared things such as, "before Abraham was, *I AM*," making himself God's equal, his hearers picked up stones to stone him.

Did Jesus not threatened those who did not accept him and his view of God's kingdom not only with the destruction by the Romans but also with the worm that never dies, everlasting darkness, eternal fire, Gehenna? One may demythologize the garbage dump Gehenna, but Jesus as a minimum promised that some Jews would be treated like garbage. Furthermore, this supposedly *nice* Jesus proclaimed that at the Last Judgment the sheep and the goats would be separated and the goats eternally punished.

In short, this so-called *nice* Jesus' words and action were so outrageous and made so many enemies that the Jewish hierarchy and the Romans collaborated to crucify him, the most horrific death for a Jew. "He who hangs upon a tree is cursed." As one perceptive theologian wrote: "Christianity is built on rock and the cross, not a hug." "His own accepted him not; they took offense at him."

Homily 33

LOSING ONE'S LIFE FOR JESUS' SAKE

"Those who lose their life for my sake will find it."

SHORTLY BEFORE MOTHER TERESA died, one of her nuns passed her room and saw her praying before the crucifix, saying: "Jesus, I have never denied you anything. You are hard."—"Those who lose their life for my sake will find it." The older I get, the more perplexed I am by Jesus' uncompromising words. "Those who lose their life for my sake will find it." Unless you hate your mother and father, you cannot be my disciple. Let the dead bury the dead. Sell all to obtain the pearl of great price. Be like the widow who gave everything she had to live on. What Jesus said to Satan in the desert about the kingdom and real life is not all about bread, making a living, or showmanship. Will Jesus say to me as he said to Peter, "Get behind me Satan."

A friend whom I admire told me Jesus died young. Therefore his uncompromising attitude, his harshness, his unbending nature, his either-or, his all-or-nothing style is typical of a young person who had not experienced many of life's contradictions. As we get older, he claimed, we become more tolerant, kind, and have learned that life without compromise is impossible. "Those who lose their life for my sake will find it."

I was initially impressed by my friend's judgment, but quickly rejected it. Not everyone grows more generous and tolerant with age. Just as I know many old, embittered, and intransient old people, I also know many young people who live Jesus' radical demands, yet are full of kindness and compassion. The gospel also stresses Jesus' mercy and gentleness with sinners. He

LOSING ONE'S LIFE FOR JESUS' SAKE

asked the adulterous woman about to be stoned, "Has anyone condemned you? Neither do I. Do not sin again." He said to the Samaritan woman at the well who had five supposedly previous husbands—"and the one you are living with now is not your husband"—and allowed her to change the subject. Jesus commands us to forgive seventy-times-seven times. Jesus is the incarnation of the Prodigal son's father, always on the lookout for his wayward son and full of love and joy when he finally returns home. When Jesus appeared to his disciples after the resurrection, he never chastised them for their cowardly abandonment.

A few months after I was almost killed when struck by a car, I awakened in the middle of one night, still very much under the influence of narcotic pain killers. Terrific hallucinations! I heard God the Father say to me: " I have denied you nothing. I am easy." I thought of Jesus saying that his burden was light and let not your hearts be troubled. "Those who lose their life for my sake will find it." I cannot say to Jesus what Mother Teresa said to Jesus: " I have never denied you anything." Purgatory is a very consoling teaching. Pope Benedict wrote of purgatory: "The fire that both burns and saves us *is Christ himself*, our judge and savior. The encounter with Christ, his gaze, the touch of his heart, the holy power of his love awakens us to the impurity and sickness of our lives. All falsehood melts away. His love sears through us like a flame, transforms and frees us, allowing us to become totally ourselves and thus totally of God. Purgatory is nothing more that our painful and healing meeting with Christ after death." "Those who lose their life for my sake will find it."

Homily 34

JESUS AND POLITICS

*"Render to Caesar what belongs to Caesar,
and to God what belongs to God."*

This morning's gospel is one of my favorites. Humberto Sousa Medeiros, the late bishop of Brownsville, Texas and then Cardinal Archbishop of Boston, was widely praised for his untiring work on behalf of Texas's migrant farm workers, the poor, and prisoners. He also opposed the Vietnam war, strongly supported busing, refused to let parents enroll their children in Catholic schools as a means of avoiding it, and spoke out against racism in certain Boston communities. But when the cardinal called abortion a horrendous crime and a deadly sin, he was severely criticized as violating the separation of church and state. The supporters of the alleged wall of separation between church and state have a special love of this morning gospel in which Jesus says: "Render to Caesar the things that are Caesar's and to God the things that are God's."

Notice the trick question of Jesus' enemies: "Is it lawful to pay taxes to Caesar?" If Jesus answered no, the Herodians would have charged him with treason against Rome. If yes, the Pharisees would have accused Jesus of disloyalty to the occupied Jewish nation and he would lose the support of the people. In asking his enemies to produce a coin, Jesus knew that the Roman coin had Caesar's graven image on it, with the inscription, *Augustus Tiberius, son of the divine Augustus and high priest*. In this way Jesus drew attention to the blasphemous image and writings and turned the tables on them. In proclaiming "render to Caesar what belongs to Caesar and to God what belongs to God," Jesus was essentially saying: "Give this filthy sacrilegious stuff back where it came from!"

Jesus' brilliant retort also echoed the slogan of the Jewish Maccabean revolt against the Syrians: "Pay back the gentiles what they deserve." When the neighborhood bully challenged me to a boxing match, my father said: "Give him what he deserves." In other words, Jesus words could have been interpreted by the subjugated Jews with respect to Caesar as: "Give as good as you get." So, his reply was ambiguous.

What Jesus did not mean was dividing human life and the world into two segments—the religious and the political. This skewed eighteenth-century Enlightenment view—bolstered by Immanuel Kant's separation of the sphere of justice from that of religion—would prevent any Christian criticism of unjust public policy, including economic policy, which is sometimes sorely needed in our world. It is often asserted that religion is a purely private matter. The mistranslated biblical text, "the kingdom of God is within you," however, better translates, as "the kingdom of God is in your midst" or "the kingdom of God is within your grasp." The Jewish people never considered the kingdom of God as a purely spiritual, private, interior relationship with God. The kingdom of God always referred to God's sovereign plan to transform the world to make everything right, and something that also happens in the public world.

Moreover, the mistranslation of Jesus' statement, "my kingdom is not of this world," more accurately means, "my kingdom is not the sort that grows in this world." The way to kingship in the ancient world was either through family lineage or by violence. For example, thirty years before Jesus' birth, king Herod the Great had defeated the Parthians, and because of Roman gratitude, he became the despised pseudo-king of the Jews.

In front of Pilate, Jesus certainly agreed that he had a kingdom—a statement that Pilate immediately seized upon—but Jesus was hardly stating that his kingdom had nothing at all to do with the present world. "Thy kingdom come *on earth*," he taught his disciples to pray. Although Jesus denies that his kingdom has such a worldly origin or quality—the world in the John's Gospel, for example, is understood as a source of evil and rebellion against God—Jesus is not denying that his kingdom is *for this world*. Jesus answered Pilate: "You say that I am a king. In fact, the reason I was born and came into the world is to testify to the truth," thereby admitting that he was in fact a king. Pilate scoffed with the question: "What is truth?"

I had a high school English teacher, who on the basis of Jesus' silence to Pilate's question, said that not even Jesus knew what truth is. This teacher, however, had no knowledge of the irony in John's Gospel. Had not Jesus said: " I am the way, the TRUTH, and the life?" Truth incarnate stands before Pilate and he does not recognize it, an example of Johannine irony.

Had Jesus preached only an interior kingdom, the religious-political establishment would not have demanded his crucifixion. If Jesus had not claimed to be the Messiah and therefore a king, Pilate would not have seen him as a threat to Rome. Neither would have the apostles Paul, Peter, and early Christians faced riots, imprisonment, and eventually the death penalty, if all they did was teaching people timeless ethical truths or a non-political, unhistoricized view of the kingdom. Like Jesus, their vision of the kingdom and future consummation remains emphatically about the transformation of this world. And this was political nitroglycerin.

Because the church exists for the sake of the kingdom of God—one of justice, peace, and freedom—the church's mission must also include responsibility for humanization in its fullest sense—activities on behalf of social justice and human rights. I had to point out to a former graduate student strongly opposed to Christian involvement in politics that this is not only justified but also mandatory because of the often *social and institutional* character of evil itself. Christianity possesses a prophetic dimension, which echoes that of the Jewish prophets who did not hesitate to castigate kings and others of authority. The struggle for social justice, peace, and human rights is an essential, constitutive duty both of the church and individual Christians.

Are we not *social* beings? Religion cannot, therefore, be a purely private matter. Love of neighbor—without which there is no love of God—requires all Christians to be conscious of their duty in the world on behalf of the dignity of the individual and in defense of justice against institutionalized injustice. Christianity's eschatological hope always entails a relativizing and the questioning of existing social structures.

To conclude, Christian faith and love have a deeply *social and political* dimension. In common with all citizens, Christians have the right and duty to participate in the sphere of public life. In the name of freedom and tolerance, Christians can rightfully demand that not only those opposed to Christian values be permitted to have a voice in the public forum. In the words of the prophet Micah, "Do justice, love kindness, and walk humbly with God."

Homily 35

MUSTARD SEED AND THE KINGDOM OF GOD

"The kingdom of heaven is like a mustard seed"

WHEN PEOPLE COME TO me for a variety of reasons, I often ask: If you had one wish, what would it be for? What is your immense longing? When I tell them that they are ultimately seeking the kingdom of God, I frequently get a puzzled look. My view of the kingdom of God was skewed for many years. When I was a child, I was convinced that the one toy I was allowed to purchase when my parents took my sister and me to the big city would make me fully happy. Soon, it was another toy, then a dog, dating the right girl, admission to college, finding a good job, entering the Jesuits, the priesthood, tenure, getting published, and so on. My often trivial sense of the kingdom of heaven.

Just a few months ago, National Public Radio had a segment on the dream of the urban Chinese. Guess what? It is the same as the so-called American dream: education, good job, good spouse, children, house, car, wealth, prestige, and so on. Does this have anything to do with the kingdom of God? What is your view of the kingdom? If you had one wish, what would it be? What is your pearl of great price? The heart is a lonely hunter, the title of a lovely novel. What does your and my heart hunt for—your and my immense longing—in short, the real kingdom of God?

One of the great blessings of my priestly and theological life was the rediscovery by scholars that Jesus must be understood as a first-century, Second-Temple, Judean Jew whose central message focused on the kingdom of God. In Jesus' day, however, the immense longing of the Jews focused on a messiah-king who would kick out the Roman occupiers, overthrow the pseudo-king Herod, rebuild the Temple, and have everyone properly observe the Law. Thus, the kingdom of God was very much of *this world*, with strong *political* overtones.

Jesus, however, emphasized that the kingdom of God was breaking in because he was present and his miracles were proof of this. He used parables to explain to his disciples what the kingdom of God is—like the small mustard seed that blossoms into the largest bush known to the Jews. Notice that Jesus did not say, "my kingdom is not of this world," but, "my kingdom is not from this world"—and has everything to do with this world. He did not say, "the kingdom of God is within you." A purely spiritual, interior kingdom made no sense to Jews. Jesus said that the kingdom of God is within your grasp. You can change the world. Thy kingdom come *on earth* as it is in heaven. Radical justice and love of neighbor have everything to do with this world. Are not those who live the beatitudes examples of what the kingdom means—for *this* world? The peacemakers, those who hunger and thirst for justice, and so on.

St. Augustine wrote that our hearts our restless until they rest in God. Is this the kingdom of God? Not quite. I am brash enough to say to Augustine that we desire to rest in God so that we can rest in our totally transformed and fulfilled selves, in the totally transformed and fulfilled selves of others, and in the totally transformed and fulfilled new creation, a creation that still groans. Only then will God be all in all! I look to the risen Christ as the seed of the new creation, the kingdom of heaven. I see in the risen Christ the proof that our immense longing will be fulfilled. You, I, the entire creation will be raised from the dead as the new heaven and the new earth. And I know that St. Augustine would agree.

Look at Christianity's history. From a ragtag group of motley disciples, a tiny mustard seed has blossomed into a world church of over one billion believers. Carl Jung, the Swiss psychologist, said that even the psyche of the western person is Christian. And time does not permit me to go into how much Christianity has changed the world for the better. "To what shall we compare the kingdom of God?"

Homily 36

JESUS FORGIVES SINS

"Who is this who even forgives sins?"

THE CONTRAST BETWEEN THIS morning's first reading and the gospel is striking. It requires the prophet Nathan's bold confrontation with king David—"You are the man!"—to awaken him to his sin of adultery and of the cowardly murder of his loyal military man, Uriah the Hittite. David repented, however: "I have sinned against the Lord." The Lord forgave him and spared his life, but his child would die. Although the Scriptures are silent about the court intrigue that went on after this, more than one scholar has noted the deviousness it would have taken Bathsheba to get their second child, Solomon, to become king after David.

The sinful woman in this morning's gospel, on the other hand, seeks out Jesus, washes his feet with her tears, (many mystics see such tears as prayer) wipes them with her hair, kissed them, and anoints them with ointment—a shocking gesture to Jesus' hosts. They murmur: "Who is this who even forgives sins?" (For years, I have offered coeds I taught at Boston College one-hundred dollars to do the same to me when I am having lunch at the local Legal Sea Foods restaurant. No takers.) At Jesus' feet, the sinful woman—who is not Mary Magdalene—learns forgiveness and love. Mary of Bethany, Martha's sister, sits lovingly at Jesus' feet. Jesus' mother, Mary Magdalene, and John ponder the mystery of crucified love at the foot of Jesus' cross.

Jesus' mercy and gentleness with sinners has long impressed me. If God is love, Jesus is merciful, forgiving, and healing love in the flesh.

He asked of the adulterous woman about to be stoned, "Has anyone condemned you? Neither do I—do not sin again." The Samaritan woman at the well—"and the one you are living with now is not your husband"—yet Jesus allows her to change the subject. When Jesus appeared to his disciples after the resurrection, he never chastises them for their cowardly abandonment.

In Julian of Norwich's famous parable of the Lord and the servant, she so strongly viewed Christ as *every person* that she transformed Adam into Christ. Thus, this Adam/Christ "fell" into the virgin's womb, fell by hurrying to serve his Lord, and fell in self-emptying love on the cross. She taught that we never stand in our own eyes and we never fall in God's sight! So confident was she of God' victorious love in Christ crucified and risen that she wrote daringly that redeemed sinners will have more joy in heaven than if they had not sinned, but said that to sin more because of this is from the devil. She pointed to king David, Peter, Paul, and Mary Magdalene as examples of those whose sins were turned into honor. "All will be well" is her famous refrain.

About her well-known visions, she wrote: "And from the time that it was revealed, I desired many times to know in what was our Lord's meaning. And fifteen years after and more, I was answered in spiritual understanding, and it was said: 'you would know our Lord's meaning in this thing? Note well. What was his meaning? Love. Who showed it to you? Love. Why did he show you? Love. Why did he show you? For Love. Hold onto this and you will know and understand Love more and more. But you will not know or learn anything else—ever!'" " I have sinned against the Lord; who is this that even forgives sins?"

Homily 37

JESUS CURES THE DEAF MUTE

"He makes the deaf hear and the mute speak"

I KNOW A HIGHLY intelligent young man, born a deaf mute—ridiculed and bullied as a boy, and not only by the children of his age. If his parents had not had the resources and he the desire to learn sign language and to read lips at an early age, he would have grown up to be a social outcast. Now he is a Jesuit priest who ministers to people who suffer from the same handicap.

National Public Radio carried a moving story about a young boy stutterer who used to take his toy animals into the closet and speak to them without stuttering. His father heard him one day and decided to take him to the zoo. Speaking to the animals there cured his stuttering and now he works for a NGO in charge of endangered wild animals.

When the deaf mute Jesuit visits our community, I observe with compassion the difficulty he has understanding what some Jesuits are saying and the frustration some Jesuits have trying to understand his labored speech. I've also noticed that in our aging Jesuit community, tensions sometimes arise because of those who mumble and those hard of hearing.

The Jews of Jesus' day so despised the deaf, the mute, the blind, those with disabilities in any form that they considered such people to be bound by Satan, having no rights, and treated almost as non-Jews. Physical disabilities meant spiritual suffering and exclusion from the community. Even in our own country, it is only fairly recent that accommodations have been made for the handicapped.

This morning's gospel—and, of course, not only here—focuses on Jesus fulfilling Isaiah's prophecy heard in our first reading. Because of Jesus-Messiah, the kingdom of God has arrived—the mute speak, the deaf hear, the blind see, and the lame walk. Calling no attention to himself, Jesus takes the deaf-mute aside and cures him in private and commands the crowd not to tell anyone. However, the crowds had long marveled that Jesus taught with authority, not like the scribes and Pharisees. Thus, with authority he casts out demons and cured. I love the reaction of the crowd to this miracle: "They said, 'he has done all things well,'" echoing what God said on the sixth day when he looked over his creation, "it is very good." Jesus, as the seed of the new creation, inaugurates the new creation.

Jesus' miracles also reveal his identity as the Messiah, the son of God, the one who restores those excluded because of their infirmities to full community membership. He brings both physical and spiritual healing—just as he fed the physical and spiritual hunger of people, as we have heard the past several Sundays. Jesus had often scolded his disciples and chastised his enemies for their spiritual blindness, deafness, and muteness—a spiritual stupidity that would be eliminated for his disciples only after Jesus' death, resurrection, and their Pentecost experience. Jesus' miracles are a sign that God created a world open to his love. As the apostle Paul writes, "a world created through and for Christ and in whom all things hold together," a world in which resurrection and the new earth will have the last word.

Einstein transformed Newtonian physics; Newton transformed Aristotelian physics; Jesus' resurrection inaugurates a New-Creation physics that transforms without destroying but carries to a new level all current laws of physics because the new creation is the goal of God's initial creation. So, miracles seemingly contradict the so-called laws of nature—only as they are understood *now*.

If Jesus asked us, "do you really hear, see, and speak about what befits my true followers," I would have to reply. I'm a faithful listener of National Public Radio. I watch the BBC, CNN, and Fox news—and, I have a Facebook account. I love movies. Yes, I am not only often astonished but also influenced by media trivia and decadence. I also saw and heard Pope Francis on social media encourage a young handicapped girl to sing him a song.

I would also say to Christ, however, "you have given us this beautiful chapel in which to see the mysteries of your life in the stained glass windows, the tabernacle in which you dwell so that we can worship you and pray in silence. We also hear in this place the word of God and learn about

JESUS CURES THE DEAF MUTE

your life and deeds—and here we commemorate your Last Supper, eat your Body and drink your Blood. Here we experience this community as the mystical body of Christ. What a great blessing!"

Mother Teresa learned to see Christ in the poorest of the poor. Do we? St. Ignatius of Loyola exhorts us to see God in all things. Do we? The psalms, Saint Francis of Assisi, and many others encourage us to see and hear how all creation praises God. Do we? I have fond memories of my great grandmother telling me at many sunsets when the chirping birds were settling down for the night: "Listen! The birds are saying their prayers." So, let us at least chirp the praises of God. "He makes the deaf hear and the mute speak."

Homily 38

JESUS CALMS THE VIOLENT SEAS

"Who is this whom even the wind and the waves obey?"

My very young sister jumped off a dock into deep water and would have drowned had I not been there. I shall never forget the panicked look on her face. Think of Jesus walking on the water and calling out to St. Peter, who, impetuously, did not hesitate to walk on the water to Jesus, only to become petrified and start to sink because of his lack of faith. Afterwards, Peter and the disciples went to the local bar to calm their nerves, only to be met by Jewish authorities curious about Jesus. Peter said to them, "Jesus may be the Messiah, but he cannot even swim."

Years ago, at a beach, south of Boston, I witnessed a young man thrashing about in the wild surf. The lifeguard got to him, but the terrified man fought him off, sank out of sight, and was found dead only several days later. When at Worcester Polytechnic Institute, I used to work summers for a utility company. My colleagues and I would hire a sea captain and his boat to be taken out for deep sea fishing. One day, a storm came up unexpectedly, and the waves were so high that the boat often became almost vertical. The propeller and shaft were then out of the water, making a very strange noise. My colleagues were petrified, some sick, but I loved it. I knew the old sea captain had been out in even rougher seas. I've seen surfers in northern Oahu in waves eighty feet high! However, we have all seen the films of the horror of the 2011 Japanese tsunami as well as the New Orleans, Texas, and Florida floods.

JESUS CALMS THE VIOLENT SEAS

The Jews, being a desert people, had an ambivalent attitude toward water. To be sure, water was exceedingly precious to desert people and the living water that Moses drew from the rock at Meribah is etched in Jewish memory to this very day. But unlike their Phoenician neighbors to the north, the Jews were not a seafaring people—apart from a few Jewish fisherman who did not venture far from shore. For them, the sea symbolized the dark power of evil that threaten to destroy God's good creation and God's people.

God created the sky and land by separating them from the dark primal waters. The Psalms often speak of the creator God who rules the raging seas, commanding their threatening waves to quiet down. In the Book of Daniel, seven sea monsters are finally put to flight by one like the son of man. In this morning's gospel, we hear of Jesus assuming this very role of God's agent who rebuked the wind, and said to the sea, "quiet! be still!" To this day warning signs dot the western coast of the sea of Galilee, warning of storms that wash away cars in nearby parking lots.

What we hear in this morning's gospel, however, is that Jesus is no Jonah who tried to escape God's calling. Jesus is so confident of his mission and power that he can fall asleep on a pillow. The gospel also underscores that because he is like us in all things but sin, he can experience fatigue. The disciples are vexed. Does he not know that the boat is about to sink and take them with it? Jesus quizzically reverses the question, putting them on the spot with a remark often found in Mark's Gospel: "Don't you have any faith?" I would have scolded the disciples for forgetting their surfboards. So when Jesus rescues the disciples from a storm, we are witnessing something similar to God's rescue of the Jews in the Red Sea. The fairly recent Christian Bale *Exodus* movie has the Charles Heston version beat by a mile. God is depicted as a child and the drowning of Pharaoh's army a cinematic feat. In Jesus, God's kingdom is at hand, the same divine power that made the world in the first place, and this power is now living in and acting through Jesus.

If you become Jesus' disciples for the kingdom of God, this story becomes your story—whether you realize it or not. Wind and storms will come your way. The power of evil was broken on the cross and in the empty tomb, but there are still too many people who prove that the shrill malevolence of evil still exists. Christians—the church as a whole, local churches here and there, individual Christians—can get hurt or even killed as a result and even be part of the evil.

So, when Jesus wakes up, pray to him in your fear and anger. And do not be surprised when he turns to you, as the storm subsides in the background, and asks: "Do you not have faith?" And never forget what John's Gospel teaches: "Out of his heart flows rivers of living *water*." With this in mind, let us end by using the prayer of the venerable Bruno Lanteri, the founder of the Oblates. " I urge you to begin each day, leaving the past to the mercy of the Lord, and the future to his divine providence. Do not let yourself be troubled by anything, not even by your own failings, taking care to overcome them immediately by an act of love of God." "Quiet! Be still!"

Homily 39

JESUS FEEDS THE MULTITUDES

"Give them some food yourselves."

IN THIS MORNING'S GOSPEL we hear of Jesus retiring to a deserted place—probably to mourn the murder of his cousin, John the Baptist—with the realization that what happened to John would most likely happen to him. When Jesus' solitude is interrupted by the crowds following him, he immediately forgets his concerns, pities the crowd, and begins to cure their sick. Growing late, the disciples tell Jesus to dismiss the crowd so they can get something to eat—probably at the local McDonald's or Burger King. Jesus then surprises them when he orders them to "give them some food yourselves." They object: "All we have are five loaves and two fish." Jesus says, "give them to me." Just as God had fed his people manna in the desert, now God in the flesh, Jesus-Messiah, feeds them, in part, through his disciples, *you*—a foreshadowing of the messianic banquet.

In the delightful Danish film, *Babette's Feast* (Pope Francis's favorite film, by the way), a refugee from the counter-revolutionary bloodshed in Paris, Babette, once the proprietor of Paris's finest restaurant, finds a home cooking bland food for a dying-out, austere Christian sect off the Danish coast. No pay, just room and board. Years later, Babette wins the Paris lottery of ten thousand francs, and, out of gratitude, decides to spend her entire winnings on a feast—and I mean feast—for the small congregation on the occasion of the founding pastor's hundredth birthday. Babette here exhibits the generosity of the poor widow who put all she had into the Temple treasury—the courage to give everything for the divine bounty of the kingdom. We hired her to cook our St. Ignatius feast this past week.

During this extraordinary feast—which several upscale American restaurants in the late 1980s duplicated for about one-thousand dollars per person—the dour congregation's disdain for earthly pleasures gradually breaks down as they eat her sumptuous food and drink the delicious wines. We see old wrongs forgiven, old loves rekindled, and a mystical redemption of the human spirit settles over the table. Deeply human, sacramental, with resonances of Jesus' meals with his disciples, with the crowds, the Last Supper, and the heavenly messianic banquet. "Give them some food yourselves."

When a talented nun friend at Yale invited me to the Newman club's soup kitchen, two things surprised me: the stench of the homeless—perhaps what Pope Francis meant when he said that priests ought to have the smell of the sheep on them. Also, the anger and hostility of those being fed amazed me. The down-and-out are not always grateful for what is given them. "Give them some food yourselves."

In this morning's gospel, Jesus has the crowd recline, not sit, as they would for everyday meals, to make themselves comfortable as one did at a banquet. As customary at Jewish festival meals, the host, Jesus, took the bread and spoke the table prayer. The host then broke the bread and gave it to each guest. Jesus so acts, but also involves his disciples. Unlike the banquets of ancient Rome, which only the rich could enjoy, Jesus feeds the multitudes—all comers. It was said of the early Christians that there was not a needy person among them. The twelve baskets of leftovers underscore Jesus' intention to restore God's people, the twelve tribes of Israel. Gathering up the fragments was another fixed ritual after an ancient Jewish banquet and Jesus' disciples do this. Why was so much left over? Ever been to a banquet in which there were no leftovers? Excess is part of feasting. No stinginess. Consider the approximately one-hundred-and -eighty gallons of water changed into the best wine at Cana! The one-hour workers who gain the same wage as those who worked all day! The divine abundance in the kingdom of God.

I'll never forget the stingy ice cream cone I got in Paris while studying there. I thought the lady was going to measure the scoop with a micrometer. Then I thought about the ice cream parlor in my home town where the generous owner would heap up scoops of homemade chocolate ice cream for us kids. Divine abundance in the kingdom of God. The messianic

JESUS FEEDS THE MULTITUDES

banquet. Jesus said: "Blessed are you who are hungry now for you will be filled." When criticized that he and his disciples did not fast, Jesus simply says that you do not fast at a wedding feast.

Jesus preached the kingdom of God, the fulfillment of the creation God loves. But people have to eat too. His disciples try to separate the kingdom of God from the rest of life. Jesus destroys that separation. The kingdom of God is for all human life. I have only one complaint. I wish that Jesus would check with Roger Berkowicz of Legal Sea Foods to expand his menu. "Give them some food yourselves—and do not be stingy!"

Homily 40

THE PROPHET ELISHA AND JESUS FEEDS THE MULTITUDES

"This is truly the prophet, the one who is to come into the world."

IN THIS MORNING'S FIRST reading, we hear of the prophet Elisha feeding one-hundred people with only twenty barely loaves—very healthy bread, by the way. In this morning's gospel, however, Jesus trumps Elisha by feeding over five thousand with only five barley loaves and two fish—but no butter, no marmalade, no tartar sauce.

In a German Jesuit house of studies, I burned my toast one morning. I simply opened the window, crumbed the toast, and tossed it out for the many birds in the area. The Germans were shocked. The holiness of bread, which for many of them during the war, meant the difference between life and death. Gandhi once said: "There are people in the world so hungry that God cannot appear to them except in the form of bread." Remember the riots in Egypt when the price of bread went up once cent? Bread and the poor.

In this morning's gospel, Philip and Andrew do not know what to do about the hungry crowd, although Andrew had found a boy with five barley loaves and two fish. So they ask Jesus—what should we do when we do not know what to do? Jesus knew what he was going to do. This event must have angered Jewish authorities because it was Passover time. The people should have gone to the Jerusalem Temple to commemorate the Exodus event instead of following Jesus, who was curing the sick.

THE PROPHET ELISHA AND JESUS

That he was called "the prophet who is to come into the world" also implied that some thought that Jesus was the true Messiah. That the crowds wanted to make Jesus a messiah-king would have deeply upset the Romans, the pseudo-king Herod, the Herodians, and many other Jews in authority. Jesus, however, did not want to be a bread king. Did not Satan tempt him with bread in the desert? For any Jew, Passover, of course, evoked the unleavened bread they baked in haste for their escape from Egypt—and also the manna with which God fed his people in the desert. That Jesus "gives thanks" over the loaves also evokes for us the Eucharist, which keeps many in the church—despite the nonsense and sin that is part of the church's reality.

Jesus has the crowd recline, to make themselves comfortable as one did at a banquet, not sit, as they would for everyday meals. As customary at Jewish festival meals, the host, Jesus, took the bread and spoke the table prayer. The host then broke the bread and gave it to each guest. Jesus so acts, but also involves his disciples. His actions foreshadow the messianic banquet of the age to come, the kingdom of God. Unlike the banquets of ancient Rome, though, which only the rich could enjoy, Jesus feeds the multitudes—all comers. It was said of the early Christians: "There was not a needy person among them."

I love to cook. What a joy to see the look on the faces of my family when I made their favorite dishes or the foreign Jesuits who so liked my spicy lunches. Jesus must have also been pleased to feed the hungry. When a talented nun friend at Yale invited me to the Newman Club's soup kitchen, two things surprised me: the stench of the homeless—perhaps what Pope Francis meant when he said that priests ought to have the smell of the sheep on them. Also, the anger and hostility of those being fed amazed me. The down and out are not always grateful.

The twelve baskets of leftovers underscore Jesus' intention to restore God's people, the twelve tribes of Israel. Why was so much left over? Ever been to a banquet in which there were no leftovers? Excess is part of feasting. No stinginess. Consider the approximately one-hundred-eighty gallons of water changed into the best wine at Cana! The one-hour workers who received the same wage as those who worked all day. The divine abundance in the kingdom of God.

Years ago a superior asked me to take a visiting Jesuit to Anthony's Pier Four restaurant. When the waiter asked what I thought of the meal, I told him that my shrimp scampi should be renamed shrimp skimpy. Then

I thought of my mother's superabundant food, so overflowing at times that my annoyed Father said that she should cook in a bathtub.

The messianic banquet! Jesus said, blessed are you who are hungry now for you will be filled. When criticized that he and his disciples did not fast, Jesus simply says that you do not fast at a wedding feast. His feeding of the multitude was a sign that Jesus was ushering in the kingdom of God, the fulfillment of the creation God created and loves. And people have to eat. Many Christians try to separate the kingdom of God from the rest of human life. Jesus destroys that separation. The kingdom of God is for all human life. "Give us this day our daily bread." I have only one complaint. I wish that Jesus would google good restaurants in order to expand his menu. "This is truly the prophet, the one who is to come into the world."

Homily 41

JESUS THE EUNUCH, BARREN WOMEN, AND THE KINGDOM

"Blessed are those who become eunuchs for the sake of the kingdom of God."

TODAY'S FIRST READING DEALING with Elkanah and his wife, Hannah, reminded me of Safid, Israel, a small town of strict Orthodox Jews with a long history of esoteric Jewish mysticism, the Kabala. A New York Jewish woman in our group pointed out to me—with disdain—that most of the women we saw in the town were pregnant.

How different from this morning's first reading, with Hannah bewailing that she is barren. For a Jewish woman, then, to be barren was almost worse than death—the ultimate curse, reflecting God's supposed displeasure and holding her up to the ridicule of all, especially Peninnah, Elkanah's fertile other wife. But Elkanah assures Hannah that he loves her, gives her a double portion of his Temple sacrifices, and asks, "why do you grieve? Am I not more to you than ten sons?" (I was touched by what a Muslim taxi cab driver in Berlin, Germany told me: " I have five daughters, but I still love them all." So much for the preference for boys.) There is a happy ending: Hannah did bear a son, Samuel, whom she promised to dedicate to God as a Nazarite, who would neither drink alcohol nor cut his hair. Samuel is an important Old Testament figure: the last judge, that is, a tribal chief of Israel and a great prophet.

During landing, a pious airline stewardess sat next to me. Somehow the conversation turned to marriage, children, and celibacy. I told her that

Jesus was ridiculed, insulted as a eunuch, for not being married and having children. An unmarried Jewish man was almost the equivalent of a murderer because he did not add numbers to his people. She insisted that God the Father knew that Jesus would be killed and did not want to leave behind a widow. I told her, however, to read the seventeenth chapter of Matthew in which Jesus did proclaim: "Blessed are those who become eunuchs for the sake of the kingdom of God." The apostle Paul teaches the same in 1 Corinthians 7. It has long struck me that whenever the New Testament speaks of marriage, it also speaks of celibacy. Do not both Christian vocations support and strengthen each other?

This morning's gospel focuses on the beginning of Jesus' public ministry in the Galilee area, a hotbed of anti-Roman revolutionary activity. John the Baptist may well have been jailed and killed by Herod, not only because his criticism of Herod's marital status, but also because of involvement with revolutionaries.

Jesus' main message is: "The kingdom of God is at hand. Change your ways." Through his actions and his preaching Jesus proclaimed that Israel's history, world history, had reached its climactic moment, because he was there. Jesus did not say, "My kingdom is not of this world," but my kingdom is not from this world"—and one that has everything to do with *this world*, a world fully transformed by God's healing and forgiving love—the new heavens and the new earth of the Book of Revelation. Neither violence nor radical fidelity to Law but only justice, love, and peace will usher in the kingdom, of which Jesus is the seed.

There was a dispute on Facebook recently about whether Jesus was a rabbi. He was called rabbi, a teacher, a prophet—but he was certainly not a rabbi in the contemporary sense. A rabbi had disciples who sought him out. Jesus, on the other hand, sought out his disciples and instructed them about the kingdom, not the finer points of the Law, as the rabbis would have. In fact, Jesus was more of a preacher of the kingdom with no place to lay his head—with such a charismatic personality that Andrew, Peter, James, and John simply dropped everything to follow him—and without any hesitation. If Jesus walked into this chapel now, would you, would I drop everything to follow him? I'd be thinking: "You want me to leave my comfortable lifestyle at Boston College? My computer? My books? My community? "The kingdom of God is at hand! Change your ways."

Homily 42

JESUS AND WOMEN I

"Neither do I condemn you; do not sin anymore!"

WHEN I WAS LECTURING in Jerusalem about fifteen years ago, I got into a cab with a New York Jewish woman who attended the lectures. Two rabbis pounded on the cab and demanded that the woman get out. Orthodox Jews will not sit near women. She told them with several choice unrepeatable words: "Either get in and ride with us or find your own cab." A woman after my own heart. To this day orthodox Jews thank God daily for not being born a pagan or a *woman*. In Jesus' day, a woman was her husband's property—he could divorce her for almost any reason.

It is astonishing how many times the New Testament refers to women, especially when compared with literary works of the same period. The most striking thing about the role of women in Jesus' and the apostle Paul's life and teaching is simple: *the sheer number* of them who are there.

The Virgin Mary became the first preacher of new covenant grace when she declared, "all generations will call me blessed, for the Almighty one has done great things for me." Her cousin Elizabeth had declared her to be the mother of my Lord (Lord being the name for God in the Greek Old Testament), the reason why Mary is called God-bearer. Mary Magdalene was the first to proclaim the good news of Christ's resurrection—Christianity's essential message—and sent by Jesus to instruct the men. The Magdalene and other Jewish women disciples, including Joanna and Susanna, accompanied and financially supported Jesus' ministry.

More remarkable: Jesus touched and allowed himself to be touched, even by sinful women. The story of the prostitute washing his feet with her tears, drying them with her hair, and Jesus' strong defense of the woman against her detractors has long impressed me. Extraordinary, too, is Jesus' scandalous Sabbath healings of a ritually unclean women who suffered from a flow of blood—and of Jesus' placing his hands on the woman bent over double to cure her. He raised the son of the widow of Nain and raised Lazarus for his sisters Mary and Martha, with whom he sometimes spent his days off. Miracles for women. Women friends.

Jesus, a Jewish man, discussed theology with the Samaritan woman at the well, considered a "half-breed" in shockingly racist terms by Jews. He also drank out of her ritually unclean Samaritan bucket. (Would a KKK member drink from an African American's glass?) Despite knowing that she had five former husbands and was now cohabitating with another not her husband, Jesus still did not avoid the Samaritan woman. In fact, after pointing out her sins, he let her off the hook by permitting her to change the subject. And she became the first to evangelize a gentile town, before Peter, Paul, and other apostles.

Moreover, you will never find an instance where Jesus disgraces or belittles a woman. Among the founders of religions and religious groups, Jesus stands alone as the one who did not discriminate in some way against women. (When the Buddha learned that women were becoming Buddhists, he complained that now it would not exist as long. The Qur'an teaches that the majority of those in hell are women.) What Jesus did constitutes a break with tradition and was without precedent in the Judaism of his day.

The apostle Paul was also radical when he wrote that in Christ, there is neither male nor female. He called Priscilla, who led the church at Ephesus, a "fellow worker in Christ" and actually explained the gospel to Apollos. Paul called the woman Junia "outstanding among the apostles." Euodia and Syntyche are famous for preaching alongside Paul, who also called Phoebe a servant of the church who helped him and so many others.

Slight change of pace: the frequent references to adultery in the Jewish scriptures is probably an indication of the result of the number of loveless, arranged marriages. Although this morning's gospel is often referred to as "the woman caught in adultery," it should also be called "the men caught in hypocrisy." Interrupting Jesus teaching in the Temple area, some scribes and Pharisees cruelly bring in a woman who had been caught in the very act of adultery. The husband had probably paid off witnesses to entrap her. The scribes and Pharisees remind Jesus of Moses' command that such women be stoned. Even more deceitful, where was the man caught in the act, for he, too, was subject to stoning?

The scribes and Pharisees asked Jesus: "What do *you* say?" If he accepted the stoning of the woman, Jesus would have to face the Romans, for only they could decree capital punishment. On the other hand, if he opposed the stoning, Jesus would appear to be in opposition to the Law of Moses. Of course, this is a set up, and the woman only a pawn used by Jesus' enemies. Keep in mind that at the end of this chapter, John 8, the conflict between Jesus and the scribes and Pharisees becomes so intense that they are ready to stone him.

After a time of silence, Jesus stooped down and wrote with his finger on the ground. It was unlawful to write even two letters on the Sabbath but writing with dust was permissible. Tradition says he wrote out their sins, but Jesus' action was also a Semitic way of his calmly expressing his annoyance at someone in the wrong—the way I would doodle on the blackboard when a student was giving me a hard time. In a previous chapter, Jesus had challenged his enemies: "Which of you will convict me of sin?" Now he stood up and said to the accusers, "let the one among you who is without sin cast the first stone." Did his mother throw a stone? He stooped down and again calmly ignored them.

Jesus' answer did not condone adultery. But—he compelled the woman's accusers to judge themselves and find themselves guilty of sin. No one could pass the test, and, beginning with the eldest, they sheepishly slipped out one by one. This scene reminded me of the movie, *To Kill a Mockingbird*, when the little tomboy named Scout calls out the names of her neighbors in the mob who were about to hurt her father, Atticus. They slink away, embarrassed. St. Augustine beautifully wrote about this scene: only two were left: misery and mercy, the woman and Jesus (it sounds better in Latin.) Jesus asked: "Woman, where are they? Has no one condemn you?" Her reply, "no one, Lord." then Jesus said, "neither do I condemn you." Despite the overly romantic view of this scene by some interpreters, Jesus did say to the woman: "Go, and from now on *sin no longer*." Here is mercy and righteousness. He condemned the sin and not the sinner. Please keep in mind Pope Francis's emphasis on mercy. "Neither do I condemn you; do not commit this sin again!" Jesus, born of a *woman*!

Homily 43

JESUS AND WOMEN II

"When the set time had fully come, God sent his Son, born of a woman!"

A CAREFUL READING OF Luke's Gospel reveals that he pays special attention to women. It cannot be by accident that stories about a man are frequently paralleled with stories about a woman. We hear of an angelic appearance to Zachary and then of one to Mary. The righteous man Simeon is described at the Temple, and then the prophetess Anna. The centurion's servant at Capernaum receives healing, and then the widow of Nain's only son is restored to life—to name but a few such companion stories. The women, moreover, often show a deeper faith and love than the men. Mary's faith, with her quiet readiness to receive God's word, is greater than Zechariah's. Simon of Cyrene is drafted to help Jesus carry the cross, but the daughters of Jerusalem spontaneously mourn and lament Jesus' suffering.

One Mass gospel reading from Luke introduces us to several devoted female followers of Jesus. Strikingly, Luke even gives us names when he can: Mary Magdalene, whom Jesus cured of her seven demons; Joanna, the wife of Herod's steward, Chuza, the king's most trusted official; Susanna, about whom we know only that Jesus had cured her of some infirmity; and many others who, out of their resources, provided for Jesus and the twelve.

I have the sense that these women saw what needed to be done to support Jesus' mission—and they did it. They had learned much from being wives, mothers, and widows. Thus, they were practical people with practical wisdom. Jesus may have told the twelve to take nothing on the journey—no staff, no bag, no bread, no money, and no tunic, but these women within their families had observed, on more than a few occasions, the foibles of their sons and husbands whom they knew would need support. The women therefore decided on a more sensible approach than is attributed to Jesus—just in case the logistics for the mission got more complicated than Jesus and the eager twelve had anticipated. I am reminded of the bumper sticker, "behind every successful man stands an astonished woman." Luke never exactly calls these women "disciples," but their wordless deeds showed their pragmatic generosity and love.

Because of Jesus' counter-cultural treatment of women and the apostle Paul's statement that in Jesus-Messiah there is neither male nor female, Christian women, from Christianity's earliest days, did charitable work not open to their pagan counter-parts. Abbesses in the medieval period had more jurisdictional power than many bishops. Catholic women mystics throughout the ages often played a significant role both in church and secular life. Catholic women from time immemorial founded orphanages, hospitals, old age homes, hospices, schools, colleges, and numerous other charitable organizations. The work that nursing nuns did on the Civil War battle fields amazed even the anti-Catholic president Abe Lincoln.

The theologian Monica Hellwig wrote that in the history of the church, women, unlike male ecclesiastics, have not ordinarily had titles that inspire awe and create psychological distance. Leadership of domination was frequently not open to them. As an unintended but beneficial result, women were often in a better position to notice what was being left undone and who was being left out in the pastoral practice of the institutional church. Hellwig maintained that it was frequently women who noticed the need for the care of the poor and the sick that led eventually to acceptance of the idea that each society, each nation, is responsible for universal health care.

I think, for example, of the Dominican sisters of the sick visiting homes and even founding Calvary hospital for the care of poor and terminally ill cancer patients. The work of the Little Sisters of the Poor is salient, as is Mother Teresa's missionaries of charity! It was primarily women who began the small initiatives of schooling for the children of the poor, including the orphaned, the homeless and the handicapped, leading eventually to almost universal literacy, public school systems, and a general belief that education is a basic right for all. I fondly recall Sister Mary Paul of the Sisters of the Good Shepherd who was radio-interviewed about the new model for foster care that she had designed. The city of New York decided to adopt her model for its homes. The admiring interviewer asked: "Sister, how did you ever come up with this revolutionary plan? Sister replied, "well, really, it's just common sense."

Hellwig also emphasized that it has so often been women who have motivated concern for peace. Especially because they are mothers and see the costs of war through maternal eyes, it has been characteristic of the lives of noted Christian women to strive for peace and reconciliation of hostile parties. Their motivation has welled up from their compassionate horror of the pain and suffering and bereavement that war causes, often to those who have least stake in the outcome. One may think of Elizabeth of Hungry, Catherine of Sienna, Dorothy Day, the women's international peace quilts—I could cite more! All such initiatives were like slow earthquakes in all western society.

So, let us pray during this Mass in thanksgiving for the gifts that compassionate, prophetic, imaginative, and faithful women have brought to the church of Christ and to humanity through the ages—from the days of the Virgin Mary, Mary Magdalene, Joanna, Susanna, and their generous companions down to our own times. Let us do what decree fourteen of the thirty-fourth General Congregation of the Society of Jesus calls upon us to do: to give thanks for the leadership Christian women have given and continue to give (often through costly struggles); and in particular for the leadership of women religious who have been pioneers in so many ways in their unique contribution to the mission of faith and justice. May we be as selfless, compassionate, competent, and creative as they in our following of Christ and service of others.

Homily 44

NO ONE KNOWS THE SON EXCEPT THE FATHER

"No one knows the Father except the Son."

I STILL HAVE POWERFUL memories of my father driving ninety-miles-per-hour on a small country road to get thirteen-year-old acute appendicitis me to hospital. In excruciating pain, I asked him if I were going to die. I shall never forget the look on his face. A father's love. I also have fond memories of my niece's husband coming home from work, and immediately upon entering the door, dropping to the floor to play Barbie dolls with his young daughter. A father's love. I recently did a memorial service for the husband of fifty-three years of the proverbial girl next door who is like a sister to me. When the daughter spoke about her father, you could have heard a pin drop in the chapel. No one knows the father like the son—but in this case, it was like the daughter.

This morning's gospel centers on Jesus' claim that only he knows the Father and that only he can reveal him. Jesus realized from early on that he had the inside track on knowing who Israel's God truly was, and what the Father wanted for his people. Only a few weeks ago we heard the twelve-year-old Jesus say to Mary: "Chill out, Mom. I'm on a mission planned by my Father."

It must have saddened Jesus that other people—including the religious leaders and even his own disciples—did not have his intimacy with God. What is your image of Jesus' Father? A charming Austrian village Catholic church contains a striking mural: a crucified Jesus restraining the sword arm of a wrathful God the Father—with the world and its people behind Mary's mantel of protection. In short, an angry God the Father who demanded the bloody sacrifice of his Son who was punished in our stead. Good Calvinism, but hardly the Father Jesus revealed.

Jesus spoke of the God of Israel as *Abba*, beloved Father. No Jew would have dared to address God as *Abba* because it was too intimate. When Moses asked God his name, he was told, "I am who I am," which could mean, "mind your own business." Or, "my name is above every name." When the disciples ask almost the same question, however, Jesus speaks about the Father of the prodigal son, the beloved father, always on the lookout for his errant son, who receives the son back with full love and has the fatted calf killed calf for a feast. And because of Jesus, we "dare" to pray "our Father," our *Abba*, our beloved Father. Because of Jesus, we are allowed to cross the line forbidden to Moses. Jesus also wants us to be as perfect as our heavenly *Abba* is perfect, a beloved Father who loves and cares for even the lowly sparrows of the air.

The Bible statement, "God is love," says the most about Jesus' Father. The medieval mystic Julian of Norwich wrote: "How can there be wrath, anger, in a God who is love?" And because Jesus penetrated to the core of his Father's identity, Jesus himself dares to say: " I and the Father are one. He who sees me sees the Father." And because the Father is Love, Jesus, his beloved son, is enfleshed Love—whose very being, actions, and mission usher in his Father's kingdom of mercy, healing, justice, and love.

The rabbis taught their people to carry the "yoke of the Torah, the Law." Jesus, whom the apostle Paul understands as the goal of the Torah, asks us to pick up *his* yoke, the yoke of love, which is easy to bear. As St. Ignatius of Loyola cried out in mystical prayer: "Such a Father of such a Son; such a Son of such a Father!"

The religious leaders of Jesus' day were convinced that their long hours of Torah study and piety gave *them* special wisdom and knowledge of God. They spoke patronizingly of the accursed mob that knows not the Law. Hence, the mob does not know God. But Jesus says: No! The wisdom about God has been revealed even to "little ones." It does not require superior intelligence and great learning. The great medieval Dominican theologian-mystic, Meister Eckhart wrote, "better one master of life than one hundred masters of learning"—he himself who had great learning.

In Boston College's renowned theology department, you will find people with doctorates in sacred learning who have written many books and lectured work-wide. But I have often encountered on and off this campus many people—even atheists and agnostics—who are "theologians" according to a much older meaning of that word. They know God *by experience* and reflect him through their lives. One of the holiest people I know is an atheistic Jewish friend who has the God of compassion, mercy, forgiveness, and love in his heart—and lives accordingly.

In line with this morning's gospel, let our spirituality be more Father-centered, not praying to some abstract God, but to the God and Father of our Lord Jesus Christ, the Father who raised Jesus from the dead. As the apostle Paul teaches, "because we are his children, God has sent the Spirit of his Son into our hearts, prompting us to call out, 'Abba, Father.'"

Homily 45

HE'S OUT OF HIS MIND

"His own received him not."

WHEN I CONTEMPLATED THIS morning's readings, I thought of a holy, learned, and exceptionally hard-working Japanese Jesuit who lived here to obtain a Boston College doctorate. When he entered the Jesuits, his Buddhist family—with the exception of his sister—would have nothing to do with him. His sister told him that his many letters to his mother and father remained unopened, so he began to send them postcards. "And they took offense at him."

In this morning's gospel, when the crowd says to Jesus, "your mother and brothers are outside looking for you," Jesus retorts, "whoever does God's will is my brother and sister and mother." Thus he contrasts the faith of those who follow him with the lack of faith among his relatives and those in his home town. An African Jesuit told me that at his First Mass, a European Jesuit asked to be introduced to his family. The African pointed to the entire village and said, "these are my mothers, my fathers, my sisters, and my brothers." His native language has no separate word for uncle, aunt, cousin, and the like, which is also true of Hebrew and Aramaic. In some cultures to this day, it does not take blood to be part of one's intimate family.

When John baptized Jesus in the Jordan, an event that inaugurated Jesus' mission, the Holy Spirit descended upon him. This Holy Spirit had abandon the Jerusalem Temple when the Babylonians destroyed it. The Holy Spirit of prophecy departed later because of Israel's sin. Jesus is now

HE'S OUT OF HIS MIND

established as Israel's true Temple and *the* prophet who would usher in the kingdom of God.

Shortly before his death, the atheist Christopher Hitchens, spoke of Jesus Christ as a madman, a megalomaniac, who allegedly thought that he was *the* way, the truth, and the life. I liked what Hitchens said because Jesus is who he says he is or he is insane. This morning's gospel, for example, shows Jesus replacing *with his own law* what YHWH had commanded the Jews through Moses with respect to love, hate, the taking oaths, murder, retaliation, adultery, and so forth. "You have heard that it was said," meaning God said, yet, Jesus insists upon, "But I say to you." The prophets proclaimed, "thus says the Lord," but Jesus said, "but *I* say to you" and "amen, amen, *I* say to you," thus placing his words in a divine context. Jesus forgave sins—who can forgive sins, but God alone?

Jesus claimed to be greater than Solomon and Elijah, the embodiment of wisdom and prophecy in the Old Testament He declared that he and the Father were one, that only he had seen the Father, that he who sees him sees the Father, and that salvation is only through him. No Jew would have called God *Abba*. It was too intimate a way to address God. Jesus always prays to *Abba* this way, however, except on the cross when he quoted from a psalm, "my God, my God, why have you forsaken me?"

Because of the power of Jesus' exorcisms, his enemies accuse him of being possessed by "an unclean spirit." He retorts that they have committed the one unforgiveable sin. They fail to recognize that he is the bearer of the Holy Spirit, the Spirit of the age to come, which makes him *the* prophet par excellence! Thus Jesus claims that he was not only greater than the Temple—the heart of Jewish life—but that his very body is the Temple itself. He claims that he is greater than Jonah, the prophet. He is God's very own enfleshed Word. He claims to be greater than Solomon, the epitome of Jewish wisdom. He is God's Wisdom in the flesh. Not only does he proclaim himself to be Lord of the Sabbath but asserts that *he himself* is the Sabbath rest and peace incarnate. "Come to me, all you who are burdened, and I will give you rest."

Jesus—through his person, miracles, exorcisms, and preaching—made the highly subversive claim that the kingdom of God was breaking in because *he* was present, that he was Israel's Prophet-Messiah-King who would finally set things straight—but in the way many Jews mistakenly thought. For some the prophet-messiah-king was the one to drive out the Romans and the pseudo-king Herod and rebuild the Temple. Did not

Herod try to kill Jesus when he was only a baby? Were not the Herodians always sniffing around to get Jesus into trouble? Moreover, the Roman had crucified not only more than one messianic-king pretender but also their followers and their families.

This is the context for understanding the reaction of Jesus' own family and the people of Nazareth—fear of what the Romans and the Herodians might do to them because of Jesus' claims. On an earlier occasion, when his relatives heard about Jesus' activities, they went to take charge of him, for they said, "He is out of his mind." The teachers of the Law exclaimed: "He is possessed by Beelzebul and a Samaritan," a racial slur as provocative as the "n" world in our culture. Although Jesus' wisdom and mighty deeds astonish the people of Nazareth, he challenges them: "You will tell me, 'do here in your hometown what we have heard that you did in Capernaum.' Truly I tell you no prophet is accepted in his hometown." He reminds them that in Elijah's time only the leprous Naaman the Syrian, a foreigner, was cured. This so infuriates his hearers in the Nazareth synagogue that they seize him and take him to the brow of the hill on which the town was built in order to throw him off the cliff. But he slips away. "His own received him not." This rejection and attempted murder by some of Jesus' relatives and the good people of Nazareth, foreshadow his ultimate rejection and crucifixion in Jerusalem.

One contemporary bishop wryly pointed out that Jesus and the apostle Paul faced grave opposition, imprisonment, beatings, and execution. But wherever the bishop went, he was treated with hors d'oeuvres, cocktails, and banquets. What would you and I be willing to suffer to remain Christ's faithful disciples? Are we even capable of forgiving not seven but seventy-times-seven times, meaning always, as he asks of his followers? Are we capable of the great love that may be demanded of us to give up our life for another? The bishop's cocktail circuit looks good from here. "His own received him not."

HOMILIES ON SIGNIFICANT CHRISTIAN TRUTHS

Homily 46

THE POWER OF FAITH

"Keeping our eyes on Jesus who perfects our faith"

When I was in Hong Kong years ago, I went to breakfast very early because of jetlag. A lone Chinese Jesuit beckoned me to his table. He was a bishop who had spent years in solitary confinement when the Communists took over. I asked if I, a stupid American, might ask a personal question. "Bishop, was it your faith and Jesuit spirituality that supported you all those dark years?" With a twinkle in his eye, he said, "yes, my faith, my Jesuit spirituality—but I am also a very stubborn man." Typical Jesuit!

One of the most striking examples of faith that I personally experienced took place when a former graduate student came to the Jesuit residence at Boston College to see me. It was evident that she was pleasingly pregnant. She told me that doctors advised her to abort because the baby would be either born dead or live only a short time. With an incredible peace that only faith in the crucified and risen Lord can give, however, she and her husband had firmly decided to have the baby. A few months later, we met again. The baby had been born, baptized, and named Elizabeth. Baby Elizabeth died a few weeks later, a funeral was held, and Elizabeth was buried. Again, I was stuck by the woman's deep faith and peace.

One of Pope John Paul II's favorite texts was Luke 18:8: "When the son of man comes, will he find faith on the earth?" As some of you know, this concern of his materialized into his proclaiming the year 2013 as the year of faith. If you were asked by Bill Maher, the comedian who ridicules people of faith, what faith is, what would you reply? Maher does not know the distinction between faith and being able to express it—the same way that people in love often cannot find words for the love of their life. I maintain that faith is basically a falling in love with the triune God and Jesus-Messiah who lived, died, and was raised from the dead to bring us true life. Through faith, we throw our arms in love around our crucified and risen Lord—and follow him. This morning's second reading from the Epistle to the Hebrew urges us to "fix our eyes on Jesus, the pioneer and perfecter of faith." Notice the paradox: on the cross he cried out both "my God, my God, why have you forsaken me" and—"Father, into your hands, I commend my spirit." The paradox of faith.

During a graduate seminar, the German Jesuit theologian Karl Rahner related that during the Second World War, a woman came to see him because her two sons were being sent to the Russian front. This meant certain death. She shouted and screamed at God, "you cannot have my sons." Well, they *were* sent and they *were* killed. The woman returned to Father Rahner months afterwards—utterly peaceful. The paradox of faith.

In the Nazi death camps the Jews would secretly meet to put God on trial for their sufferings. When the time came for worship, they would cease their deliberations to praise and worship God. How strange life is; how strange faith is. Hadewijch, a thirteenth-century mystic, wrote: "Hell is the seventh name of this faith wherein I suffer. For there is nothing faith does not engulf and damn, and no one who falls into her and whom she seizes comes out again, because no grace exists there." Her statement reminds me of Mother Teresa who lived in a crucifying darkness of faith without one shred of religious emotion for almost fifty years. Her love for Jesus-Messiah and the outcasts of society to whom she ministered never wavered. She wrote, "it often happens that those who spend their time giving light to others, remain in darkness themselves (like teaching at Boston College for almost forty years). If I ever become a saint—I will surely be one of darkness. I will continually be absent from heaven—to light the light of those in darkness on earth." How often does faith require living in darkness! Karl Rahner wrote that faith means a lifetime of putting up with God's incomprehensibility. I would go further. Faith means wrestling not only with God's incomprehensibility but also with *our own incomprehensibility*, our own mystery. As the intriguing mystic, Ramon lull, wrote, "the human person is an abyss whose bottom is the abyss into which even the soul of Christ vanishes." Let us pray with the Jewish father who brought his possessed son to Jesus and begged: " I do believe. Lord, help my unbelief."

Homily 47

SUFFERING FOR THE KINGDOM OF GOD

"Christ had to suffer and to rise from the dead, and so enter into his glory."

This morning, as with many first readings during this Easter season, we hear that as the early Christian movement spread rapidly after Jesus' resurrection many Christians had to suffer and at times endure cruel deaths to enter the kingdom of God. After the apostle Paul was struck blind during his encounter with the risen Christ, he was instructed to go to Damascus where he would meet the disciple Ananias. Jesus had told Ananias: "Saul is a my chosen instrument, to bear my name before the gentiles and kings and the sons of Israel; for I will show him *how much he must suffer for my name's sake.*"

We just heard about Paul left for dead after the crowds stoned him. He had said of himself: "Five times I received thirty-nine lashes. Three times I was beaten with rods, once I was stoned, three times I was shipwrecked. I have been on frequent journeys, in dangers, dangers, dangers." A Buddhist once told me that the apostle Paul would have not made a good Buddhist because of his *anxiety* for the churches. I told him to reread Paul and to note Paul's great *joy* in serving Christ crucified because he was *worthy* to suffer for Jesus-Messiah. Apostolic suffering is a salient feature of his epistles.

An American bishop, with a sense of humor, told me that wherever he goes, there are banquets and tea parties—not the riots and sufferings Paul faced. I am always amused by what Annie Hall in the Woody Allen film said. "If the enemy threatened to take away my credit card, I would confess to anything." What are you, what am I willing to suffer for the gospel? In some parts of the contemporary world, Christians must suffer much for their faith. I would have difficulties giving up my computer.

Because of the crucified and risen Christ, St. Teresa of Avila wrote, "Let nothing disturb you. God alone suffices." Jesus says in this morning's gospel that he gives us peace, but not as the world gives it. The American author, Walker Percy, wondered why Christians—given the gospel's good news and the Easter event—were often so gloomy and depressed. The human mess!

In this morning's gospel, Jesus speaks of the devil, the ruler of the world, coming—a foreshadowing of his crucifixion, which would prove to be Jesus' definitive exorcism of the evil one. On the cross, he would break the devil's power. Notice how after Jesus' agony In the garden, he goes to his suffering and death with *deep peace*. "Peace be with you," messianic peace, psychosomatic wholeness, the effect of doing God's will.

I have known very holy Jesuits, suffering much for their vocation, whose inner peace radiated from them. I just returned from one of the most difficult trips in my life. I wish that I could say that I had the peace Jesus-Messiah spoke about. My mantra: "The stress be with you." If only we could be Christian gyroscopes. No matter what you do to a gyroscope, it says fixed at its still point. If we stayed rooted in the crucified and risen Jesus-Messiah, then our lives would be different, filled with a peace and joy that the world cannot give. Peace, the peace of the messianic age, when all things will be fulfilled—but have begun to be fulfilled in the risen Jesus-Messiah. His peace be with you!

Homily 48

PRAY UNCEASINGLY

"Pray always without becoming weary."

JESUS, A FIRST-CENTURY, SECOND-TEMPLE, Judean Jew, certainly prayed with his people and also in private. Moreover, Jesus, Mary, and Joseph prayed the rosary together every evening—and did the Stations of the Cross every Friday. Jesus often spent the entire night in prayer. He prayed in the desert for forty days where he did battle with Satan. He taught his disciples the Our Father prayer and also that certain demons are driven out only by *prayer* and fasting. On the night he was arrested, he was praying In the garden of Olives—the subject of so much art and music. Mel Gibson's controversial movie, *The Passion of the Christ,* offers an astonishingly powerful and beautiful portrayal of Jesus' garden agony—to my mind, one of the greatest scenes in cinematic history.

Jesus' entire being *is* prayer—one big YES of worship and adoration of the Father. And—as the enfleshed Word, he is God the Father's prayer to us. Cardinal Pierre de Bérulle, the seventeenth-century French mystic-theologian, wrote that because of Jesus, the God-man, Christianity has not only a God ador*ed* (the Father) but also a God ador*ing* (Jesus).

Today's gospel instructs us to pray always without becoming weary. The apostle Paul also urges us to pray without ceasing. Biblical text after text after text urges us to pray. St. Monica prayed weepingly for years for her son Augustine. One mystic wrote that to weep is to pray, if done for the sake of God. I have a very holy priest friend who complains that because of physical sufferings, he cannot pray. I told him that suffering *is* prayer, *if* one is united to Jesus-Messiah. "Be still and know that I am the Lord," proclaim the Scriptures. My mother's neighbor took care of his Alzheimer's wife for over ten years, a love that is definitely anonymous prayer. Dying to self daily for Jesus-Messiah, in whatever form it takes, is the prayer of everyday life.

Prayer is not only intimate conversation with the triune God whom we can address as Thou—a profound grace—but it is also is the fundamental act of human existence. To pray is *to be* in the most profound sense of that word. I would argue that in prayer we not only speak to God but also that God speaks *us to ourselves*. Have your ever noticed that we talk to ourselves a good part of the time? What do you say to yourself in this inner dialogue? It is instructive *what* we say to ourselves. Break that inner dialogue and pray to the Father, the Son, and to the Holy Spirit.

When Michael Caine, the outstanding British actor, was in New York to speak with his agent, he saw on TV a lovely Brazilian model advertising Maxwell House coffee. He said to his agent: "I'm going to Brazil to find that woman and marry her." His agent informed him that she worked in a New York modeling agency and that he would get her phone number. Caine called her for a date every day for weeks. She always said no. One day, after almost losing patience, he called again. Bingo. A date—and they have been married for over forty years. "Pray without becoming weary!"—the secular version.

When an interviewer challenged Karl Rahner, the German Jesuit theologian, because of his great faith despite the horrors of Nazism, he replied: "I believe because I pray." Moreover, "one can rightly say that at least some of those condemned human beings went to the gas chamber praying and believing in God." Not a few people have told me that they do not need Sunday Mass because they are good people. In one case, I found out later that the person needed a kick in the butt and an exorcism, not prayer. We should go to Mass to be *thankful*, eucharist means thanks, to pray, to worship, to adore, and to love the triune God. When someone tells me how good he or she is, I know that they are not.

When in the Middle East I was always impressed by how Muslims would drop everything in order to *pray* either privately or publicly five times daily, a powerful symbol of our creaturehood and dependence upon God. How many of our churches are empty, except perhaps on Sundays?

During an interview, Pope Francis spoke of his prayer routine: the breviary every morning, his love of the Psalms, Mass, the rosary. He suggested briefly pondering the mystery and then saying the decade. The Pope related that he prayed when waiting for an elevator, for a train, at the dentist. He loved the evening hour adoration in front of the Blessed Sacrament—even when he got distracted or even fell asleep praying. He imagined himself as an old dog sleeping at his master's feet.

The Buddha taught: "I have gained nothing from meditation, but lost anger, anxiety, depression, insecurity, fear of old age and death, and gained peace." There is scientific evidence that people who pray have better physical and mental health. I liked what Pope Francis said about his prayer being full of memory. "I look at my life and ask, with St. Ignatius, 'what have I done for Christ? What am I doing for Christ? What should I do for Christ?' With Ignatius, gratefully I recall the many gifts that I have received, and try to find God In all things.'" The prayer of gratitude!

St. Teresa of Avila wrote that prayer "is nothing else than an intimate sharing between friends and taking time frequently to be alone with him whom we know loves us." When asked how he prayed, the Curé of Ars said that in chapel he looked at Christ and Christ looked at him. My father had the morning offering prayer taped to his shaving mirror. I have a Jesuit friend who always carries a pocket New Testament with the Psalms and prays the Scriptures whenever possible. I've seen people on the transit system prayerfully reading the Scriptures.

Many prayerful people like to sit in the presence of the Blessed Sacrament and recite the Divine Praises or short prayers, in rhythm with their breathing—trying like the hawks that fly around campus—not to flap the wings of their reason too often. A priest gave bad advice to a woman of deep prayer when he erroneously said that he could not help her with prayer because she sat in the presence of the Blessed Sacrament and did nothing. When one loves, presence *is* often the only thing necessary. Whatever works. "Pray always without becoming weary."

Homily 49

BE RICH IN WHAT MATTERS TO GOD

"Vanity of vanities; all things are vanity."

This morning's three readings all deal in some way with inheritance and greed. As a chaplain at Mercy Hospital in San Diego, I witnessed—in their dying mother's room—a son and daughter fight about who would get what. The daughter implored me to convince her brother that the mother had promised her the clock and other things. I was too young and polite to quote Jesus, "who appointed me as your arbitrator?" In one bitter divorce, I was prevailed upon to decide who would get the Thanksgiving turkey platter—after thousands of dollars had been spent on lawyer fees. I said that I would buy them both a turkey platter. In my many years of priesthood, I have seen not only many families shattered over inheritance matters but also parents who worked intelligently and diligently pass on their large or small nest eggs to their children only to have it squandered in a very short time. "Vanity of vanities; be rich in what matters to God."

When in Warsaw, Poland, I befriend a Polish university professor who had been fired because of his anti-Communist stance. I accepted his offer of a city tour, during which he sarcastically pointed out what he called Warsaw's new cathedral: a huge shopping mall, a place he said that now had more worshippers than the main cathedral. When Mother Teresa was taken to a large mall in the U.S.A. and shown all the wonderful things available, she said: "Yes, it is all very beautiful, but I need none of it." She was a woman who did not despise the good things of life but was especially rich in what matters to God. I, however, would have taken Mother Teresa to the Apple Store and asked: "Are you certain that you do not need the new twenty-seven inch power iMac, three-point-eight gigahertz processor, quad core, thirty-two gigabytes of ram, special sound and graphics card?" I love computers. My vanity of vanities. The greed that is idolatry.

Why do we have such a hunger for more earthly goods than we need and forget about being rich in "what truly matters to God?" Recent surveys indicate that because of the pandemic lockdown, many people are spending even more on line for things they do not need. The first temptation was to be like God, who is all and has all. We often seek to quench our deepest desire, the immense longing, with more and more power, honor, entertainment, alcohol, drugs, sex, iPads, iPhones, and the like. You name it. Greed comes in many forms and nothing satisfies our immense longing. As St. Augustine wrote, "Our hearts are restless until they rest in Thee."

Jesus was a man truly rich in what matters to God. As the God-man, he reveals not only who God is—"he who sees me sees the Father"—but he also reveals what it means to be a genuine human being. "He who sees me sees the new Adam," the transformed human being. The famous German Jesuit theologian, Karl Rahner, emphasized that Jesus was a first-century Judean Jew—and certainly uneducated by the Roman and Greek standards of his day. Unnoticed for most of his life, unmarried, he led a short public life as a wandering preacher for whom everything in a certain sense was already dead, or at most provisional. He considered the seemingly necessary and beautiful things of life unessential to his mission, which was to be and to usher in the kingdom of God. He died the death of a common criminal on the cross—but was raised from the dead.

I would emphasize, however, that unlike John the Baptist, Jesus was no ascetic and certainly did not despise the good things in life. How often do we find Jesus at banquets, wedding feasts, and sharing a meal with his disciples, sinners, and the outcasts of society. He wore good clothing, the seamless garment the crucifying soldiers did not want to tear—and he enjoyed a day off with Martha, Mary, and Lazarus. His first miracle consisted in changing about one-hundred-eighty gallons of water into a fine wine. Did the original wine run out because Jesus and his disciples had arrived?

When my mother was dying in hospice, my niece wisely suggested that we—family and friends—have Mass at the foot of her bed. My mother was rich in the things of God, but still had the petty vanities and petty attachments we all do. It struck me forcefully during Mass at the foot of her bed that only through death and purgatory would she be *totally* rich in the things of God. "Vanity of vanities; be rich in what matters to God."

Homily 50

THE LORD'S PRAYER AND AGING

"This is how you are to pray"

MANY OF THE EARLY church fathers called the Lord's Prayer a summary of the Gospels. The Pharisees, Essenes, John the Baptist, and other individual Jewish religious groups were marked by their own prayers and customs. Jesus here teaches his disciples to how to pray. In this context, the Lord's Prayer is not that of an individual but of a community. Although a favored Christian prayer, Jesus is hardly teaching the Our Father as the only way to prayer. He prayed in his own way throughout the night, in the desert, and in the garden—often silently, often using the Jewish beloved psalms, sometimes expressing his feeling in his own words. The apostle Paul instructs us to *pray* always. Do *you* pray? How do you pray?

Jesus had cautioned his disciples against babbling like pagans thinking that they will be heard because of their many complicated magical words. Note that the Lord's Prayer is a thoroughly *Jewish* prayer. You can find all the phrases in Jewish world prior to Jesus. Even today, a pious Jew could pray the Our Father. A Jewish man prayed with me when he was severely injured in an automobile accident.

This deeply meaningful prayer is set within our calling God *Father*, as Jesus did. This Father longs to see his sovereign and saving rule, his kingdom, become fully present *on earth*—not for God's people to be snatched away from earth to heaven but for the glory and beauty of heaven to be turned into *earthly reality* as well. The prayer reminds us of the prophet Ezekiel's prophecy that there would come a time when God's *holy name* would be praised, not abused by invading armies. The Jews took seriously the identity between a person and his name. The next part of the prayer echoes God feeding his people in the desert and now Jesus giving us his body and blood as food. Moreover, we must pray for the good of the entire world, where millions starve daily.

We pray for forgiveness with the realization that to be forgiven one's faults and sins is an indescribable gift. How difficult it is to forgive. Jesus also teaches of a time of testing, as he would be tested during his passion. If we follow a crucified Messiah, we too should not expect to be spared periods of darkness. Finally, we pray to be delivered from evil both in its abstract and personified form, the evil one himself.

I wish now to say something briefly about prayer and aging. Karl Rahner made much of the fact Jesus died young. He was spared the trials and tribulations associated with old age. Rahner wrote that old age is a vocation not given to everyone. When Jesuits are sent to retirement homes, they are missioned to "pray for the Society of Jesus."

I know French and a few of the African Jesuits here became upset when I called them *jeune chien*, young dog. To be called a dog in Africa is an insult. Jesus told the Syrophoenician woman that one does not throw bread to the dogs—one of Jesus' harshest statements. I told the Africans that *dog* can be a term of affection and from then on they called me *vieux chien*, old dog.

I was amused during novitiate when an elderly Jesuit giving us a retreat said that he often fell asleep during prayer, like an old dog at his master's feet. Some of the overly zealous novices were shocked. Pope Francis gave a long interview in which he discussed his prayer life and confessed that he often fell asleep during prayer. True love allows the loved one to fall asleep in his or her presence. I have always liked what the Curé of Ars said about prayer before the Blessed Sacrament. I look at Jesus and Jesus looks at me. The Scriptures teach: "Be still and know that I am the Lord."

My answer to my superior's question about my prayer did not amuse him. I said: " I show up. Moreover, after all these years I sometimes say to Christ: 'All right, I've been doing all the work over the years, now it is your turn.'" Saying this to older nuns in a homily, however, did amuse them. They know that prayer can be hard work.

Karl Rahner wrote that prayer is the fundamental act of human existence. It is the profoundest symbol that we are created and loved by God. To be able to say *Thou* to God is a precious gift. To be able to address Jesus'

Father as *Abba*, beloved Father, is also a great grace. Teresa of Avila defined prayer as intimate conversation with the one we love and who loves us. Rahner also wrote that prayer is the last moment of speech before silence; the act of self-disposal just before the incomprehensible God disposes of one; the act of letting oneself fall—after the last of one's own efforts—into the infinite fullness and silence that reflection can never grasp. When challenged by an interviewer because of his great faith despite the horrors of Nazism, Rahner said: " I believe because I pray. I pray because I believe. I also believe that despite the horrors of Nazism, some concentration camp inmates went to their deaths praying."

When you pray, do you pray to the Father as Father, the God and Father of our Lord Jesus-Messiah, the God who raised Jesus from the dead? Do you pray to the Son as Son and to the Holy Spirit as Holy Spirit? Do you pray not to an abstract Jesus but to the Jesus crucified and risen, the Christ who was in the womb, born, a child, a teenager, and a young man? His entire past was taken up into his risen life, just as our past lives in us now. "This is how you are to pray."

Homily 51

PARABLE OF THE WEDDING FEAST

"How is it that you came in here without a wedding garment?"

THIS WEEKEND, MY CONNECTICUT niece's college son comes home for the first time and will bring two of his college friends with him. The playful affection between him and his sister has long amused me. Mel Gibson's controversial film, *The Passion of the Christ,* offers a wonderful depiction of the love and playful affection between Jesus and his mother. Devoted son that he was, Jesus practiced his sermons and parables in front of his mother. Because Mary found Jesus' parables difficult to understand, she regretted having sent him to Jesuit schools.

When Mary listened to this morning's parable about the king who gave a wedding feast for his son, she asked, "Who is this king?" Jesus replied: "my heavenly Father, the God of Abraham, Isaac, and Jacob." "Why a wedding feast," she asked? "well, mother, if you had listened to this morning's first reading from Isaiah, you would know that I am speaking about the messianic banquet." "Watch your tongue, son! You may be the Messiah but I am still your mother."

Mary asked: "Who are these servants sent out with the invitation and why were they ignored, mistreated, and even killed?" "These servants, mother, are the prophets my heavenly Father sent again and again. They were ridiculed, treated badly, and sometimes killed because too many of our people have had hearts of stone. The poor prophet Jeremiah, for example, complained bitterly about what he suffered to be God's prophet and even proclaimed, "would that my mother's womb had been my tomb."

PARABLE OF THE WEDDING FEAST

Then Mary asked: "To what does this refer: *the enraged king whose troops killed the murders of the prophets and destroyed their city?*" "Well," Jesus said: "Jeremiah, for one, was correct. The Babylonians not only destroyed the Temple and leveled Jerusalem, but they also took most of our people into exile. Have I also not warned Chorazin, Bethsaida, and Capernaum for rejecting my teaching about the kingdom of God? Have I not wept over Jerusalem and warned them about the impending destruction by the Romans because they too reject my teachings?"

Then Mary asked: "Who are these servants sent out to the highways and byways to invite the good and even the bad to the wedding feast?" Jesus replied, "those are my disciples in imitation of me." "Did I not go to the Little Sisters of the Poor in Somerville, the Poor Clares of Jamaica plain, the Franciscans sisters on Center street, the holy ones in neighboring nursing homes, and seek out the good who attend Mass at Boston College? Do I not eat with the good at Legal Sea Foods and the Cottage Restaurant at Chestnut Hill?"

"The bad? Well, I eat with the worst Boston politicians on Beacon Hill. I've had many meals at McDonald's and Burger King with the prostitutes who frequent the Combat Zone. And for the really bad, I go to the cheap bars around Boston College, especially the dive, Marianne's. Those BC students and the Jesuits who teach them—bad news! And because I eat and drink with the good and the bad to symbolize that my heavenly Father invites everyone to the messianic banquet, I am accused of being a glutton, a drunkard, and a friend of sinners. Some say that I am out of my mind."

"Jesus," Mary asked: "What about the guest without a wedding garment who gets tossed out into the darkness?" "My apostle Paul," Jesus replied, "instructs my followers to *clothe* themselves with compassion, kindness, humility, gentleness and patience and over all these virtues to *put on* love." Paul also reminds us that all who were baptized into Jesus-Messiah have *clothed* themselves with him. Did you not put a white garment on me when John the Baptist baptized me? Everyone may be invited, but entrance into my Father's kingdom is not automatic. I expect the invited to change their ways."

"Speaking of wedding garments," Mary said, "we are invited to the O'Brien wedding in Cana next month and you need new clothing. You look like that shabbily dressed Jesuit who walks the Chestnut Hill reservoir." "All right," Jesus said, I'll go to Mr. Goldfarb, the Nazareth tailor." When Jesus and Goldfarb met, Goldfarb said: "Jesus, when I get through with you,

you're going to like the way you look." Jesus asked, "How much?" Goldfarb retorted: "Far be it from me to charge the Messiah. Anyway, it's good publicity to be known as the one who clothes the Messiah."

Jesus was a big hit at the Cana wedding feast not only for changing water into wine but also because of his extraordinary wedding garment. Goldfarb received so many orders for new clothing that he made a business proposal to Jesus. "Jesus, your foster father Joseph is dead; your mother is getting old. Come work with me and you will make a much better living for your mother and you than carpentry. We'll call our business *Goldfarb and Jesus*."—Jesus thought and then said: "All right, but we are going to call it *Lord and Tailor*."

Homily 52

A WORTHY WIFE

"When one finds a worthy wife, her value is far beyond pearls!"

During summer breaks from engineering studies at Worcester Polytechnic Institute, I worked for the Connecticut Light and Power Company. I became lifelong friends with one of the office staff who was exceptionally good to me. A few years ago, his wife of over fifty years contracted Alzheimer's and, when institutionalized, my friend drank and starved himself to death. Real life more powerful than the profound love of man and wife in the excellent movie, *The Notebook*. I've known and know numerous people married thirty, forty, fifty, and even seventy years who have definitely become one flesh and thanked God for it. When I visited my aunt, whose husband for fifty-two years had died, she said, "How I miss my *friend*." I was amused when I jokingly chided a Boston College workman for holding hands with wife of over forty years and she replied: "Well, we *love* each other." "When one finds a worthy wife."

When working as a chaplain at San Diego's Mercy Hospital, I went into the waiting room to call in the family of a dying sea captain as I anointed him. The eldest son told me to take only his mother. As I began to anoint the man, his wife of over fifty years very lovingly grabbed her dying husband's arm, totally ignored me, and said to him: "I've always loved you. Thank you for being such a good man, husband, father, and grandfather. Thank you for the children and grandchildren you gave me and for the long life we shared. It breaks my heart, but now I give you to God. I'll see you in heaven." The son later told me that they had met at a church dance the day the father had pulled into port. They married the very next day. "When one finds a worthy wife."

In that same hospital I walked into the intense care unit to find a man cursing his unconscious, dying wife: "You bitch. I hope that you are suffering. You are the worst thing that ever happened to me. Go to hell." I guided him out and realized that he was undoubtedly the worst thing that had ever happened to her. "When one finds a worthy wife."

The Book of Genesis contains the profoundest words ever written about the blessings of a good wife. God said, "It is not good for the man to be alone. I will make a helper suitable for him." But nothing God created was found suitable. So God caused the man to fall into a deep sleep and took one of the man's ribs and made a woman from the rib and brought her to the man. Archie Bunker of TV fame maintained that God made Eve out of an inferior cut of meat! But just remember that Adam was made from the dust of the earth. Now when Adam saw the woman he said ecstatically: "This is now bone of my bones and flesh of my flesh; she shall be called 'woman,' for she was taken out of man." This is a Semitic way of saying, "wow, this is terrific!" Was this the source of the serpent's envy? The rib symbolizes that woman was not made from man's head to top him; nor out of his feet to be trampled upon by him, but out of his side to be *equal* with him, under his arm to be protected, and near his heart to be loved.

Furthermore, the first blessing in the Bible is on man and wife. Their *one flesh* is seen as primordial life-giving complementarity and communication. The social critic, Camille Paglia is spot on when she wrote that "it is women's superior biological status as magical life-creator that is profaned and annihilated by the barbarism of sex crime. The gender ideology dominating academe denies that sex differences are rooted in biology and sees them instead as malleable fictions that can be revised at will." This view is another reason the church is so strict in matters sexual and marital.

Was not Adam and Eve's surrender to the serpent's envy the beginning of the friction between them and of the blame game? As one of my Jesuit friends claims, the relation between man and wife can sometimes be like a card game that begins with two hearts and ends with a club and a spade.

One of my former graduate students was quite taken when I taught that one should marry a sacramental person, one in whom you find God and will lead you deeper into God's mystery. She told me that when she first gazed upon her husband's nakedness, she wept with joy: a healthy female response. C. S. Lewis's marvelous book, *Screwtape Letters*, contains a letter from the senior demon Screwtape to his nephew Wormwood. Screwtape despised women who remained virgin until marriage and then gave themselves to their husbands fully and joyfully. "And that is why a man leaves his father and mother and is united to his wife, and they become one flesh." In a powerful Indian film, the husband—upon hearing of his brother's sexual abuse of one of his daughters—falls to his knees and sobbingly clings to his wife. "Therefore shall a man leave his father and his mother, and shall *cleave* unto his wife: and they shall be one flesh," the King James translation, which I like.

Adam named his wife Eve, because she would become the mother of all the living. The Word became *flesh*, born of a *woman*. The number of times in the course of history the church has had to protect the dignity of marriage, the holiness of bodily love. The eccentric but holy fourteenth-century hermit-mystic, Richard Rolle, wrote: "There is a certain natural love of a man toward a woman, and of a woman towards a man, from which no one is free, not even the saint. It was instituted by God in the beginning according to nature, by which they dwell together, and in concord with one another, and make one another happy socially by natural instinct."

When the Pharisees challenged Jesus for his views on divorce, he replied: "Because of the hardness of your hearts Moses allowed you to divorce your wives, but from the beginning it was not so." Male and female were created "in God's image and likeness." "What therefore God has joined together, let no man put asunder." This view challenges both the acceptance of divorce and of same-sex marriage. In saying this, Jesus places woman on a par with men. In Jewish culture women had no rights. To this day, orthodox male Jews pray daily: "I thank you Lord for not being a gentile, a slave, a woman." On the other hand, many rabbis view circumcision as a warning to the man to treat his wife well.

Think, moreover, of the acid attacks and the so-called honor-murders of women and wives in some parts of the world. I found instructive the horrible way women are treated in Khaled Hosseini's *A Thousand Splendid Suns*, based on his first-hand experience of the Taliban. Even in contemporary India, the saying to some women is: "Your husband is your tomb." I would add that this is true not only in some parts of India.

The apostle Paul exhorts men this way: "Husbands, love your wives, just as Christ loved the church and gave himself up for her. Husbands ought to love their wives as their own bodies." Even more apposite, the apostle wrote: "There is neither Jew nor gentile, neither slave nor free, nor is there male and female, for you are all one in Jesus-Messiah."

The famous tombstone in Logan, Utah of the cowboy Russell Larsen reads: Five rules for men to follow to have a happy life: 1) It is important to have a woman who helps at home, cooks, cleans up, and has a job. 2) It is important to have a woman who makes you laugh. 3) It is important to have a woman you can trust, and does not lie to you. 4) It is important to have a woman who is a good bedmate and likes to be with you. 5) Finally, it is very, very important that these four women do not know each other or you could end up dead like me. As the Book of Proverbs states: "The man who finds a wife finds a treasure and he receives blessings from God."

Homily 53

CHILDREN AS GIFT AND CELIBACY

"Hagar bore Abram a son, Ishmael"

THIS MORNING'S FIRST READING focuses on the rivalry between the allegedly infertile Sarah—who would later give birth to Isaac, Jesus' forefather—and the taunting maidservant, Hagar, who gave birth to Ishmael. Both Hagar and Ishmael were eventually driven out, because Isaac was to be the seed of the covenant between God and his people.

As I prayed over the text, I thought of the mighty warrior Jephthah the Gileadite, who had promised God that if he were victorious against the Ammonites, he would sacrifice the first Israelite he met on his way home. The unfortunate person turned out to be his daughter. She told him to fulfill his vow but also to allow her to spend two months in the mountains to mourn her virginity. When some students snicker when I tell this story, I remind them that for a Jewish woman to be barren was the ultimate shame and, in some ways, a living death—the ultimate curse, reflecting God's supposed displeasure, and holding her up to the ridicule of all. This is still true in some parts of the contemporary world.

And Sarah so suffered until she gave birth to Isaac in her old age. The only positive statement we find in the New Testament concerning infertility is when Jesus prophesies Jerusalem's approaching doom. Jesus' woeful beatitude: "Blessed are the barren, the wombs that never gave birth."

I know a marvelous woman at Boston College who was told by doctors that she would never have children. The sheer joy on her face when she exclaimed to me that one morning—after seven years of marriage—she discovered that she was pregnant. She now has two lovely children. Years ago a former graduate student came to see me. It was evident that she was pleasingly pregnant. She told me that doctors advised her to abort because the baby would either be born dead or live only a short time. With an incredible peace that only faith in the crucified and risen Lord can give, however, she and her husband decided firmly to have the baby. A few months later, she met with me again. The baby had been born, baptized, and named Elizabeth, another gospel woman supposedly barren. Baby Elizabeth died a few weeks later, a funeral was held, and Elizabeth was buried. That young woman's faith touched me deeply.

Contrast this with a woman I knew who used to date my best friend. She told me privately that she would never marry him because he wanted children and if she ever became pregnant, she would commit suicide. Most men and women normally have a natural desire for marriage and to have children. Pope John Paul II called this the "spousal meaning of the body"—that all human persons, by their very nature, are intended for the spousal gift of self to another in love and in a way that brings forth new life. I've known many infertile couples who spent much time, money, and endured much pain and discomfort for fertility treatments.

So, is it not paradoxical that the incarnation totally bypassed one aspect of the spousal meaning of the body? Mary remains a virgin; Jesus never marries. Jesus was ridiculed, insulted as a eunuch, for not being married and having children. An unmarried Jewish man was almost the equivalent of a murderer because he did not add numbers to his people. With respect to something foreign to human nature, Jesus proclaims: "Blessed are those who embrace celibacy for the sake of the kingdom of God." The apostle Paul was also celibate and taught: "I say to the unmarried and to widows that it is good for them if they remain even as I."

We know that those called to celibacy for Jesus-Messiah and his kingdom, like those invited to marriage, are called to the spousal gift of self to another and to be fruitful, but to give life in a *spiritual* way. St. Thérèse of Lisieux describes her profession of vows as her "wedding day" and that her religious life would result in many *spiritual* children. Many saints and mystics also spoke of their *spiritual fecundity*.

So, in tune with this morning's readings, be we married, single, or celibate for the sake of the kingdom of God, let us rejoice in our vocations and for the new life we bring into this world.

Homily 54:

CHILDREN: THE GREATEST IN GOD'S KINGDOM

"Who is the greatest in the kingdom of heaven?"

WHEN I READ AND prayed over this morning's gospel, I thought of Mohammed Ali who used to brag: "I am the greatest." Many football fans would consider Tom Brady to be the greatest. I like tennis and favor the great Novak Djokovic. The Olympics? Who will emerge as the greatest? Phelps? The current political scene: the greatest? Trump? Macron? Merkel? Putin? We all want to be the greatest.

When the disciples asked Jesus who was to be the greatest in God's kingdom that was to come on earth, we are probably right to suppose that they had their Israelite heroes in mind: Abraham, Moses, David, Solomon, the great warriors of their past, the Maccabees, and the like. The first thing I thought of when I read this morning's gospel focused on Jesus' appreciation of children was a video of child soldiers in Africa training with a Kalashnikov assault rifle, a deadly but easy to use, weapon. I also thought of Boko Haram and ISIS—their kidnapping of young girls to be sold as sex slaves. Of Malala, the Pakistani girl, shot in the head because she wanted to go to school, the youngest person ever to receive a Nobel peace prize. I also thought of the rich and spoiled children growing up in the western world, needing more electronic gadgets to keep them amused and the children in Africa hired to work with dangerous chemicals to extract the previous metals from our thrown-away electronic goods.

It is significant that in Greek, the language of the New Testament, the words for child are neuter: the child is simply an *it*. This is true of contemporary German, *das Kind*, neuter. For the Israelites, children were only semi-human and had no rights. The child in this morning's gospel I suspect is a girl, not least because a girl would forcefully make the point Jesus was wanting to get into his disciples' minds. Namely, that the weakest, most vulnerable, least significant human being you can think of is the clearest possible signpost to what the kingdom of God will be like. God's kingdom—the future time when heaven rules completely *on earth*—will not be about the survival of the fittest. It will not be the result of some long evolutionary process that the strongest, the fastest, the loudest, the angriest people get in front of everyone else.

Jesus tosses all that out the window, and instead calls out a little child: shy, vulnerable, unsure of herself, but trusting and with clear eyes, ready to listen, to be loved, to love, to learn and grow. This is what true greatness is like, he says. His disciples, all relatively young men, must have found it difficult to think that weakness and vulnerability are anything other than something to be ashamed of. I suspect that most contemporary Americans feel the same way. Of all the major world religions or philosophical anthropologies, however, Christianity alone emphasizes that even in the womb the child is a *human person*. For this reason, the church protects and has reverence for the child at *every* stage of its development. The Russian philosopher-writer Dostoevsky wrote that the soul is healed by being with children. And Jesus said about children, "to such as these belongs the kingdom of God."

Homily 55

JULY FOURTH—INDEPENDENCE DAY

"They confessed that they were strangers and foreigners on the earth seeking a homeland. But as it is, they desire a better country, that is, a heavenly one."

I BEGAN A FOURTH of July homily one year with the words: "God damn America; God bless America." America was the first nation founded as the embodiment of an idea—the "self-evident" truth that "all human beings are created equal" and endowed *by God* with an "inalienable" right to life, liberty, and the pursuit of happiness—in a world that had always connected nationhood and citizenship to blood, soil, and ethnicity. Incredible!

American history is replete, however, with violations of its own Declaration of Independence: slavery, the near-genocide of the native American population, racism to this day, the deep divide between the haves and the have-nots, and so on. These evils have deeply scarred the American psyche. "Irish need not apply," right here is Boston. The lesser known exploitation of Chinese immigrants, who built so much of this country, and then were kicked out.

When quite young, I saw the Ku Klux Klan burning a cross on a far-off hill in my home town in north-east Connecticut, a burning aimed *not* at African Americans but at *Catholics*. One definitely low point in American history was the horrific fire bombings of Japanese cities and then the atomic bombs dropped on Hiroshima and Nagasaki. The dark side of the American soul.

On the other hand, consider the statue of liberty: "give me your tired, your poor, your huddled masses yearning to breathe free; the wretched refuse of your teeming shore, send these, the homeless, tempest-tossed to me. I lift my lamp beside the golden door!" America can be proud that it has *often* lived up to its promises to be a beacon of hope and the land of opportunity and plenty. The shrill disputes over immigration policy, however, are still part of the national fabric.

Most countries celebrate their independence day with military parades and other shows of force. We celebrate with barbeques, small town parades, fireworks, the Boston Pops, and tall ships in the harbor. President Obama's first inauguration profoundly moved me: our first president with African roots; the crowds, a stirring example of true diversity and respect for the other.

I lived in divided Berlin, Germany for six months and was blessed with the experience of spending time behind the Iron Curtain, Russia, and Soviet bloc countries. I saw first-hand the darkness and oppression. I love supermarkets and cannot help thinking of the empty East-bloc stores whenever I am in Shaw's or Whole Foods.

America and her allies saved western Europe and a *pax Americana* has endured for over seventy years. Japan, Germany, and South Korea are prosperous and democratic, thanks to the U.S.A. Shipping on the Atlantic and Pacific oceans are duty-free, thanks to the United States. Former president Bush was called a Nazi by a Boston College Jesuit, only to be chided by our mainland Chinese Jesuit who said that in China the insulting Jesuit would be hauled off to a re-education camp. God bless America.

Jesus must be understood as a first-century Judean Jew who clearly loved his country, his people, and knew both the good and evil that filled their history. He wept for his people who did not know that only he and his Father give true peace and freedom. Jesus' person, mission, and preaching focused *not* on universal love, as one often hears, but on the kingdom of God that was breaking in because *Jesus* was present. Israel's history—our history—had reached its climactic moment, Israel's dream—our dream—was coming true right then and there.

Jesus did *not* say, "my kingdom is not of this world," but my kingdom is not *from* this world," and has everything to do with *this* world. Jesus died and rose from the dead so that a nation, all nations, and this world will die and rise as the kingdom of God, the new heavens and the new earth.

JULY FOURTH—INDEPENDENCE DAY

Thy kingdom come! Come, Lord Jesus, come. God bless America and teach us what gives true peace and freedom!

Homily 56

REJOICING IN THE ANNIVERSARY OF MY JESUIT VOCATION

"If anyone comes to me without hating his father and mother, wife and children, brothers and sisters, and even his own life, he cannot be my disciple."

THE MORE I STUDY and contemplate the gospels, the more paradoxical and controversial I find our crucified and risen Lord, Jesus-Messiah. Almost nothing was more important to the Jews of first-century Judea than family—and, of course, one's own life. Do you hate your family and your own life? Certainly, some harsh biblical statements are for emphasis and not to be understood literally.

Without in any way denigrating marriage, Jesus also praises those "who have made themselves *eunuchs* for the sake of the kingdom of heaven." Jesus' enemies called him a eunuch—a slur—because a Jewish unmarried man was not a real man—and, almost as evil as a murderer because he did not propagate, increase the number of his people. Even Jesus' own family said of him: "He is out of his mind."

On a personal note: the front cover of a 1958 *Saturday Evening Post* has a photo of a scowling Jesuit general, with the caption: "The black Pope—obeys no man on earth except the Pope." The hyped article described the Jesuits as the "pope's commandos," who, unlike monks, use the entire world

THE ANNIVERSARY OF MY JESUIT VOCATION

as their place to pray. Shortly thereafter, I quit my electrical engineering position at Boeing in Seattle and entered the Society of Jesus.

Exactly fifty-three years from yesterday, my father—with my mother and sister—drove me to the Jesuit novitiate in the Berkshires, where I was to embrace Jesus' injunction to follow him by becoming not only a pope's commando but also a Jesuit eunuch. Exactly fifty-one years ago today I took my simple vows of poverty, chastity, and obedience. Exactly thirty years ago here at Boston College, I took my solemn vows.

Jesus speaks of the hundredfold given to those who leave everything to follow him. Since this is my anniversary, please permit me to be somewhat personal by enumerating some of that hundredfold. First, I was blessed with an incredible thirteen-year Jesuit education, which culminated in a doctorate from a German university. Second, I've been to Asia, Africa, North and South America, Europe, and Australia. Penguins do not listen to Jesuit lectures, so that leaves Antarctica out. Third, what of intimacy? I performed a wedding last weekend for the daughter of a man I taught at Holy Cross some over fifty years ago. The groom's father spoke movingly and lovingly about waking up daily at his wife's side for almost fifty years, the greatest blessing of his life. He told his son that he would now have that joy with his new wife.

I have a confession to make: this Jesuit eunuch would have loved being a husband and father—and everything that that implies. I've always liked women (I'm not supposed to say that, but I have a vow of celibacy, not blindness) and I've always liked children. When I entered the Jesuits, women in my hometown threw themselves off cliffs like so many lemmings.

However, there are many forms of intimacy. I live, pray, dine, recreate with Jesuits from much of the U.S.A., Australia, Europe, Africa, India, Malaysia, Vietnam, Korea, and even mainland China—right here at Boston College. They are some of the holiest, emotionally integral, intellectually awesome people I know. They live what Jesuits are all about, companions of the trinitarian Christ whose lives are filled with the selfless service of others. One of our General Congregation document states that "there were men who lived quietly and unknown, and men who were renowned scholars, preachers and teachers; men who laid down their lives for the gospel, for the church, for the poor; men who lived simply and faithfully in a world that never understood their poverty, chastity, or obedience; men who brought society to this moment. We give thanks to God for them."

On another note, this Jesuit eunuch—for over forty years—has not only taught students but also heard their confessions, married them, baptized their children, buried their grandparents, and parents, and in a few cases, them. People—and not only Catholics—confide in me—in some case, more intimately than with their own spouses.

In prayer, day after day and year after year, I gradually fell more and more in love with the crucified and risen Jesus-Messiah and the triune God who indwells me. Daily Mass for me is never routine but an intimate entry into the mystery of Christ's salvific work. When I baptize a baby or adult, hear confessions, marry people, perform funerals, preach God's word—I am astonished at the power of Christ grasping me intimately through the church's liturgy. This intimacy differs from that resulting from marriage and children, but it is a profound intimacy no less.

Shortly before Mother Teresa died, one of her nuns passed by her room and saw her praying with arms outstretched, saying to Christ crucified: "I have never denied you anything. You are hard." I wish that I could say what Mother Teresa said. While recovering from an accident that almost claimed my life, heavily sedated, I awakened in the middle of the night to hear the God and Father of our Lord Jesus Christ say to me: "I have never denied you anything. I am easy."

Thus on this anniversary day, I can say: although I went through the turbulent sixties and seventies—when so many of my friends were leaving the priesthood—I've never looked back. I love being a Jesuit eunuch and I love my priesthood. And to paraphrase the apostle Paul in his Letter to the Philippians: "I have absolutely no regrets about what I gave up because of the surpassing worth of knowing Christ Jesus my Lord."

Homily 57

RETHINKING PURGATORY

"Depart from me, Lord, for I am a sinful man."

WHEN I WAS IN my first year teaching at lovely Santa Clara University many years ago, a student said loud and clear during a class in which the topic of sin arose, " I have never committed a sin in my life." If I were a fire and brimstone cleric, I could have hurled at him John's First Epistle: "If we claim we have not sinned, we are calling God a liar." Or when Jesus said to those about to stone the woman taken in adultery: "He who is without sin cast the first stone."—Do you know what he said when a stone came flying in? "Mother, stop that." So, I simply asked this gentle, confused, and definitely a psychedelic drug user: "You say that you never committed a sin? Is your mother still a virgin?"—a joke that only some in the class got.

Well, we are all sinners. I like what Pope Benedict wrote in his encyclical on hope: "For the great majority of people, . . . in the actual choices they make, despite a deep openness to love, to God, in the depths of their being, *filth* also covers their love. However, the thirst for love remains and constantly re-emerges from the filth that remains present in the soul." When people die, few can stand before the triune God and Jesus-Messiah without stinking at least somewhat. The Book of Revelation states it clearly that "nothing defiled can enter the new Jerusalem." This accounts for the church's ancient practice of praying for the dead and its teaching about purgatory.

My mother used to ask, whatever happened to purge-a- tory (sic)? I know all too many Catholics, even priests who should know better, who ridicule the notion of purgatory. But I take this fact as seriously as does church tradition and official church teaching. In the Russell Crowe version of the *Robin Hood* film, in gratitude for returning the sword of his fallen knight son, the old, blind Sir Walter Loxley said to Robin Hood: "Pretend that you are my son returned from the Crusades. Please stay to protect my daughter and me. Dinner shortly, but first take a bath— you stink."

That Christ throws his arms around all who die into him and invites them to the messianic banquet, I sincerely believe. Unlike the stench of the sheep Pope Francis urges us to have, however, those who stink of disorder and sin in any way face a purgative bath. Did not a six-winged angel apply a *purgative* hot coal to Isaiah's unclean lips and say, "your sin is taken away." Consider St. Peter who on one occasion painfully exclaimed, "depart from me, Lord, for I am a sinful man." Many a saint and mystic have *excruciatingly* uttered those words because of the agony of disorder and sin in the presence of holiness.

Even when I was in college and before I entered the Jesuits, if I were out for the evening with the car, my mother would sleep on my bed until I came home. She wanted to be certain that I was all right, but it also kept me on the straight and narrow. I hardly wished to pain my mother with any wrong doing. The often purgative experience of interpersonal relationships.

St. Ignatius—and he was not the only saint—suffered an *earthly purgatory* when the remembrance of past sins so tortured him after his dramatic conversion that his self-hatred led him to contemplate suicide. When I first arrived at Boston College, a young woman I knew had been converted by charismatic Christians from a life of drugs, alcohol, and sex. However, she suffered painful psychosomatic ailments for years. Garbage in, excruciating garbage out.

When in college, a friend and I took our motorcycles for a ride through curvy, country back roads. I took a curve too fast, crashed, and road burned the left side of my body, leaving it with bloody open wounds pocketed with sand and grit. Later, an amused family doctor cut off some of my clothing, poured surgical soap on the wounded areas and scrubbed them with a surgical brush—and gave me nothing to kill the pain. Then he said: "If that was fun, then you will love this," as he poured an antiseptic on the just-scrubbed areas. I thought that I was on fire. An earthly purgatory. Garbage in, garbage out painfully.

What of a recovering alcoholic, a recovering drug user, a recovering smoker, or a recovering over-eater? An earthly purgatory awaits them. One

RETHINKING PURGATORY

example: when running up Heartbreak Hill years ago, I saw a woman bent over vomiting and in much pain. She told me that once she began to have children, she let herself go—eating, drinking, and smoking more and more. Now, dieting, giving up smoking, drinking moderately, and exercise, she experienced her earthly purgatory. Garbage in—painfully purging garbage out.

In the section on purgatory in Pope Benedict's encyclical on hope, he writes of the testing fire of which Paul wrote in 1 Corinthians 3:10–15: "The fire which both burns and saves us is Christ himself, the judge and savior. . . . The encounter with Christ is the decisive act of judgment. Before his gaze all falsehood melts away. . . . In the burning, transforming, and freeing pain of this encounter, when the impurity and sickness of our lives become evident to us, there lies salvation. His gaze, the touch of his heart heals us through an undeniably painful transformation 'as through fire.' But it is a blessed pain, in which the holy power of his love sears through us like a flame, enabling us to become totally ourselves and thus totally of God." Mom, that is what happened to *purge-a-tory*. "Depart from me, Lord, for I am a sinful man."

Homily 58

RETHINKING HELL

"Depart from me, you who are cursed, into the eternal fire prepared for the devil and his angels."

MICHELANGELO'S SISTINE CHAPEL CEILING artistically immortalized the Gospel of Matthew's Last Judgment. The angels separate the children of the kingdom—God's holy people—from the evildoers, Boston College students, and the Jesuits who teach them—and toss them into the fiery furnace.

The well-known Anglican C. S. Lewis once wrote that every person we meet is someone, who, if we saw them now as they will be in the age to come, we would be strongly tempted either to worship them or to recoil from them in horror. The sheep and the goats, two very different types of human beings. Take for example the infamous Nazi, Heinrich Himmler, the architect of the holocaust and one of history's most successful mass murderer. Even Himmler's face, his body language, radiated evil. A lesser known Nazi, Ilse Koch, often referred to as the "Bitch of Buchenwald," used her sexual prowess by wandering around the death camp naked, with a whip and a pistol, to shoot any man who so much as glanced at her. She would also select inmates with interesting tattoos to be killed, so that their skins could be made into lampshades for her home.

In a chilling movie, *The Prisoners*, the woman, with a gun pointed at the father looking for his missing daughter, explains that after her young son died of cancer, she and her fundamentalist preacher husband went around kidnapping and killing children to turn their parents into demons in order to get even with God. People who create hell on earth. Is it any wonder that many a thinker has written of such demonic people as charred stones who were once human beings, as un-persons who despaired about life's ultimate meaning, as those consumed by their own terminal narcissism and hatreds? Now contrast that with the holiness and light emanating from the face of Mother Teresa or good Pope John XXIII. The goats and the sheep.

The few times that I have broached the subject of eternal punishment, hell—either in lectures or in graduate seminars—have occasioned either irritation and/or scorn. The cover and editorial of the Christmas issue of the British *Economist* years ago ridiculed the Christian notion of hell by depicting it as a demon-filled place of eternal tortures in the style of Hieronymus Bosch or Albrecht Dürer—unfortunately, an all-too common view of both those who reject and those who accept the teaching of eternal punishment. David Bentley Hart's recent book, *That All Shall Be Save*, jeers at the very notion of hell and accuses a tradition of "loving hell" for nefarious purposes. Although I too reject popular notions of hell, anyone who takes the Scriptures and the church's long tradition seriously faces an unsettling mystery: the New Testament is replete with references to the possibility of eternal punishment—and the fact remains: *there will be a final judgment. We shall be judged!*

I find it fascinating, however, that the long-standing traditional belief that few will be saved shifted in the twentieth century to the orthodox question: Can we *hope* that everyone will be saved? No less than the *Catechism of the Catholic Church*, popes John Paul II and Benedict XVI emphasize, in according with 1 Timothy 2:3-5, that God wishes the salvation of all, that Christ was crucified and raised from the dead to confirm the triumph of good over evil. Where sin abounds, grace abounds all the more. Their teachings affirm the *hope* that no one will be lost from the community of the saints.

I find it instructive and consoling that the church has declared certain persons to be *saints* but has never said *definitively* that so and so is in hell, even though an unofficial tradition certainly has Judas, Nero, and others as undergoing eternal punishment. And not a few contemporary people would assert this of Hitler and other monsters of history.

That said, I would maintain that an orthodox contemporary theology could understand hell as the eternally loving *presence* of God, Christ, angels, saints, animals, vegetation, and material creation to the damned, the eternally obdurate, whose obstinate use of their freedom and raging hatred of and fury at the holy and the good have rendered them incapable of receiving and responding to this loving presence. The gates of hell, so to speak, are locked from the i*nside*. The damned damn themselves, *if* any do so.

Edith Stein, now St. Teresa Benedicata, the Jewish Carmelite nun wrote that although God respects human freedom, he may outwit it. The apostle Paul wrote: "Who shall separate us from the love of Christ? I am convinced that neither death nor life, neither angels nor demons, neither the present nor the future, nor any powers, neither height nor depth, nor anything else in all creation"— I would add, even our own hardness of heart—"will be able to separate us from the love of God that is in Christ Jesus our Lord."

Homily 59

JAIRUS'S DAUGHTER: CHRISTIAN PESSIMISM AND OPTIMISM

"Our savior Jesus Christ destroyed death."

THIS MORNING'S HOMILY FOCUSES first on Christian pessimism, death, and then on Christian optimism, resurrection. When I looked at the monitor in my father's hospital room after he had suffered two heart attacks, I asked the surgeon, "he's brain dead, isn't he?" The surgeon said yes, so I said, "please take him off life support." He was reluctant, but I insisted. I knew my father. I called in the family, and as he breathe his last, we prayed him from this to the next life. A painful but also a blessed experience. The sting of death.

I received an email recently from a former German Jesuit friend with whom I studied in the early seventies. He left the Jesuits, married, and I've known the wife and family for over forty years. About twenty years ago they found their eldest son hanging from a tree—no explanation. Just a few years ago, their youngest son was killed in an automobile accident. They are trying to make sense of it all. The sting of death.

This morning's first reading insists that God did not make death, but that it entered the human condition because of the "devil's envy." Is not death truly the most shattering event in human life? How much pain, anxiety, and suffering are connected with it! How often does death, especially of one's loved ones, call into question life's very meaning. Thinkers from time immemorial have claimed that death contains all human mysteries in itself. It is the point at which a person becomes a radical question to himself or herself. In the Swedish director Ingmar Bergman's masterpiece, *The Seventh Seal*, a knight returning from the Crusades, must play chess with Death to save or lose his life. At one point, he says to Death, "If there is nothing beyond you, then you are God."

What nonsense that our skewed culture spends so much time and effort denying death. It astonishes me too, how many people, even Catholics, now have no liturgy or ceremony to commemorate the passing of the loved one to eternal life. However, we die. Even Jesus died. Google, for example, "paintings of the dead Jesus Christ." Some are utterly shocking. As Christians we confess that the fundamental event of the history of salvation and of the world is the death of Jesus Christ on a cross. Has the death of any other historical figure been subjected to such scrutiny?

The paradox: death is seemingly natural—everyone and everything dies. Yet, it is also experienced as unnatural, as something that should not be. We know on one level that we are going to die, but in reality, I think that Freud was correct when he wrote that we cannot imagine our own death or represent it to ourselves. No one really believes in his or her own death. In their unconscious, everyone is convinced of their own immortality. Christian pessimism, however, teaches that death has indeed the *next* to the last word.

Part two, and a link to today's gospel: When in high school, I used to help the slightly younger girl across the street with her algebra. One afternoon, she went riding with another couple and her boyfriend—no drugs or alcohol involved—the car crashed and she died. The mother never got over it. What a crushing experience to lose a child. The sting of death.

This morning's gospel focuses on another dead young girl, Jairus' daughter, whom Jesus resuscitated. He throws out the ridiculing crowd, brings the father and mother into the room, takes the twelve-year old child by the hand, and says: "Little girl, I say to you arise!" And she does. The line I love, "Give her something to eat."

John's Gospel emphasizes that Jesus is *the life* who resuscitated Jairus's daughter, the son of the widow of Nain, and Lazarus. Resuscitation, however, returns a persons to ordinary life and they must die again. Resuscitation is not resurrection. The scriptures also inform us that we all die in Adam and will all live through Christ, that Jesus rendered the devil, the lord of death, powerless. Christians experience Christ's victory over death

CHRISTIAN PESSIMISM AND OPTIMISM

by sharing in it, especially through baptism and the Eucharist, which is a foretaste of the resurrected life. And because of Jesus' victorious resurrection, the apostle Paul can rejoice: "Where, O death, is your victory? Where, O death, is your sting?"

Christian optimism is based on the fact that because of our crucified and risen Lord, Jesus Christ, forgiveness, love, and transformed life have the last word—not sin and death. I, we, the entire cosmos shall be raised from the dead to be the new heavens and the new earth. "Our savior Jesus Christ has destroyed death."

HOMILIES FOR THE FEAST OF SAINTS

Homily 60

THE CALL OF THE APOSTLE MATTHEW

"Jesus said to Matthew: 'follow me.'"

In an interview that made headlines Pope Francis spoke of his frequent visits to the Roman church of St. Louis of France to contemplate the striking Caravaggio painting, *The Calling of St. Matthew*, inspired by today's gospel. Pope Francis related: "Jesus looked at Matthew—whose name means 'Gift of God'—with feelings of mercy and love, chose him, and said, 'follow me.' That finger of Jesus pointing at Matthew, points at me. I feel like Matthew. It is Matthew's gesture that strikes me. He hold on to his money as if to say, 'No, not me! No, this money is mine.' Here, this is me, Francis, a sinner on whom the Lord has turned his gaze."

My first main point: notice the irony in today's gospel. Matthew is in a toll booth, probably collecting taxes on the fish leaving the sea of Galilee area. The Jewish people despised tax collectors because only the highest bidders obtained their position, which was to extract taxes from their countrymen to line the pockets of the hated Roman occupiers. Moreover, most tax collectors were known for overcharging so that they could skim money off the top. Thus, they were not only collaborators with the despised Roman conquerors but also corrupt—even the Romans scorned them.

Think about this for a moment. Matthew had a rather cushy job, was certainly married—with wife, children, and an extended family. It is fairly certain that he possessed land. However, Matthew responded to Jesus call, "Follow me," without hesitating. The gospel says that he got up and left everything for an unstable life as a follower of a wandering prophet. (I would have asked Jesus if I could take with me my iMac, iPad, books, and the like).

In St. Ignatius's *Spiritual Exercises*, the apostle Matthew is the paradigm of devout persons who are so moved and attracted by Christ's call that "without hesitation, or the possibility of hesitation, they follow it." The second main point: the Pharisees immediately demean Jesus because he ate with tax collectors and sinners. Unlike our fast food culture, Jews viewed table fellowship as something intimate, as an act which bound them not only to each other but also to God. No fervent Jew, therefore, would have eaten with tax collectors, thieves, prostitutes, brawlers, drunkards, peasant farmers, Boston College students, the Jesuits who teach them—anyone who could not or would not live a full life faithful to Jewish covenant traditions.

Please remember that Jesus was not an ascetic, such as John the Baptist. He frequented cheap bars in promulgating the kingdom and was called a glutton, a drunkard, a friend of deplorables. Jesus' table fellowship with outcasts—with anyone who shared his view of the kingdom—was, therefore, a *subversive* prophetic action that not only indicated that the messianic banquet of the kingdom of mercy and forgiveness had begun because Jesus was there. But it also prophetically dramatized that the Jews of Jesus' day had a false view of what the kingdom of God was.

The third main point: when Jesus quoted the prophet Hosea: "I desire mercy and not sacrifice" and said that he came to call sinners, he was in effect judging the beloved Jewish Temple to be irrelevant, redundant because God's mercy and forgiveness were given through him—the presence of the kingdom—not through ritual purity and the animal sacrifices performed there. In fact, because of Jewish national fanaticism, Jesus predicted that the Temple would be destroyed. Jesus did more than cleanse the Temple—he doomed it because Israel would not change her ways. Again, Jesus acts and speaks as God's *subversive prophet* by undermining cherish Jewish belief.

Today's lesson: Let as be quick, such as Matthew, quick to follow Jesus' prompting, seek him for your peace, mercy, and forgiveness. He is our true Temple. As he said to Matthew, "Follow me."

Homily 61

PETER THE PARADOX

"Blessed are you Simon, son of Jonah. For flesh and blood has not revealed this to you, but my heavenly Father"

WHEN I MADE MY first thirty-day retreat as a Jesuit novice in 1960, the contemplations involving St. Peter were often the most powerful. Thus, I've long had much devotion to this remarkable man. Second only to Jesus, Peter is the most mentioned person in the New Testament. And like Jesus, Peter was a Jew. So when we Christians reverence Peter, we are reverencing our own Jewish roots. As Jesus himself says in John's Gospel, "salvation is from the Jews."

When the New Testament writes about Peter, there is almost always a linkage between something strong and positive about him and something negative and weak. This morning's gospel indicates that because of God the Father, Peter was the first to recognize that Jesus was much more than a prophet—he was in fact the "Son of the living God." However, Peter the rock—a play on words because the Greek word for rock and Peter are the same—becomes such a stumbling block to Jesus' mission that Jesus calls him "Satan," a term that Jesus did not even call his enemies. And blustery Peter called out to Jesus on the Sea of Galilee: "Lord, if it is really you, tell me to come to you across the water"—and he takes a few steps and starts to sink. Likewise, just before Jesus' agony in the garden, Peter loudly proclaims that he would lay down his very life for Christ. But all too quickly, Peter denies him three times. "I know not the man."

I love the story of the risen Christ's appearance on the lakeshore. The Beloved Disciple—always quick to recognize Jesus—says, "it is the Lord." Without hesitation, splash, Peter is in the water, so eager to see Jesus. At breakfast when asked by Jesus three times if Peter loves him, Peter painfully blurts out: "Lord, you know everything. You know that I love you." Months later, in Antioch, Peter eats and drinks with gentiles. People show up from James in Jerusalem to chide Peter for eating with gentiles, and he chooses the cowardly way out. The apostle Paul rebukes him to his face. Later, Peter has his famous food vision in which God reprimands him: "What God has cleansed, do not call it unclean."

If we are committed to Jesus, but sometimes too scared to live out that commitment, Peter is a saint with whom we can we can identify. And if Jesus did not give up on Peter, then we can be certain that Jesus will never give up on us. I think of Peter for the dimension of weakness and disorientation that haunts almost everyone's life. Let us take the ancient tradition that he moved from Jerusalem to Antioch and then from Antioch to Rome. This is Peter the Galilean fisherman, whose accent made him sound like a rube in Jerusalem. He probably knew some Greek because some Jews in that area did. But try to imagine Peter conserving with the better educated Jewish and gentile Christians of Antioch or Rome. I think he must often have had difficulty understanding what the people around him were saying, and that once he understood the words they were saying, he must often have wondered what they meant by those words. And the same would apply to anyone he addressed. And at the end, caught up in the persecution under Nero, he confessed that he was not worthy to die as Jesus did, so he was crucified upside down.

As my community and I get older, community members and I often do not know what is going on due hearing loss. So, I think of Peter, and pray Thomas Merton's prayer: "my Lord God, I have no idea where I am going. I do not see the road ahead of me. I cannot know for certain where it will end. Nor do I really know myself, and the fact that I think I am following your will does not mean that I am actually doing so. But I believe that the desire to please you does in fact please you. And I hope I have that desire in all that I am doing. I hope that I will never do anything apart from that desire. And I know that if I do this you will lead me by the right road, though I may know nothing about it. Therefore I will trust you always though I may seem to be lost and in the shadow of death. I will not fear, for you are ever with me, and you will never leave me to face my perils alone."

Homily 62

PETER WALKS ON THE WATER

"Lord, if it is you, command me to come to you on the water."

IN THIS MORNING'S FIRST reading we hear of Elijah on stormy and noisy Mount Horeb experiencing God as a *tiny whispering sound*. But on the stormy sea of Galilee, the frightened fishermen disciples encounter Jesus walking on the water, and like the creator God of the Old Testament, he is very much in control of nature. The gospel does not tell us this, but after this ordeal, the disciples headed to the nearest fishermen's bar only to find there Pharisees, Sadducees, and priests drinking and eager to find out about Jesus. The disciples tell them, "He's the Messiah and he cannot even swim?!"

When I made my first thirty day retreat as a Jesuit novice years ago, the contemplations involving St. Peter were some of the most powerful. Thus, I've long had much devotion to him. Second only to Jesus, Peter is the most mentioned person in the New Testament. When the New Testament writes about Peter, however, there is almost always a connection between something strong and positive and something negative and weak. Like many of us, he is the disciple of love and faith, mixed with fear and doubt.

In this morning's gospel, blustery Peter calls out to Jesus on the stormy Sea of Galilee: "Lord, if it is you, command me to come to you on the water." Jesus says: "Come on in, the water's fine!!" Peter takes several steps, panics, and starts to sink. "Why did you doubt, you of little faith?" Peter was also the first to recognize that Jesus was much more than a prophet, confessing him as the "Son of the living God." Peter the rock—a play on words, Greek for rock is *Petra*—becomes such a stumbling block to Jesus' mission that Jesus calls him "Satan," a term that Jesus did not even call his enemies. Likewise, just before Jesus' agony in the garden, Peter loudly proclaims that he would lay down his very live for Christ. but all too quickly, Peter denies him three times. "I know not the man."

I love the story of the risen Christ's appearance on the lake shore. The Beloved Disciple—always quick to recognize Jesus—says, "It is the Lord." Without hesitation, splash, Peter is in the water, so eager to see Jesus. Painfully during breakfast he confesses: "Lord, you know everything. you know that I love you." And we know of his later cowardice when he refuses to eat with gentile Christians. But like Jesus, Peter was a Jew, as were all Jesus' disciples. So when we Christians reverence Peter, we are reverencing our own *Jewish* roots.

The late Henry Ford, the founder of the Ford Motor Company, had such a hatred of Jews that he wrote a book arguing that Jesus was not a Jew. Many Enlightenment scholars had also attempted to dissociate Jesus from his Jewish roots. Jesus Christ, with Christ as a proper name, is another way of obscuring Jesus' radical Jewish identity. He is Jesus-Messiah, the long-promised anointed one of *Israel*. During a dinner with some who denigrated the Jews, St. Ignatius of Loyola shocked his guests when he said that he wished he were Jewish in order to be related to Jesus by blood. Ignatius also had a great desire to live and work in the Holy Land in order to walk in Jesus' footsteps.

One of the great blessings of my life resulted from those scholars who show without a doubt that Jesus was a first-century, Second Temple Judean Jew who saw himself as the consolation of Israel, *the* Messiah foretold by the prophets, as the one who would bring Israel's history as God's chosen people to be the light of the world to its victorious conclusion. And Jesus emphasized: "Salvation is from the Jews."

This morning's second reading is a small segment from chapters in which the apostle Paul asks: "Has God rejected his people? By no means." Paul then boasts of his Jewish heritage and writes "of those of my own race, the people of Israel: theirs is the adoption as sons; theirs the divine glory, the covenants, the receiving of the Law, the Temple worship and the promises. Theirs are the patriarchs, and from them is traced the human ancestry of Jesus-Messiah." He reminds the Roman gentile Christians, who tended to dislike Jews—that they are grafted on to Israel, the olive tree whose root is holy and that the hardening of the Jews brought them great blessings.

PETER WALKS ON THE WATER

If you read the letters of the apostle Paul properly, you will notice how Paul rethinks Israel's entire history in the light of the crucified and risen Christ and the Holy Spirit. Paul understood Jesus-Messiah as the fulfillment and transformation of Israel's entire history, especially of the promises God made to Abraham: "You are my chosen people." Christians are of Abraham's seed, the renewed Israel—not the replaced Israel—in the crucified and risen Jewish Jesus-Messiah and his Holy Spirit that enables us to call God, *Abba*, beloved Father.

As early as 1938, Pope Pius XI said that Christians are spiritual Semites. Pope St. John Paul II, who made headlines in 1986 as the first pope to visit Rome's main synagogue, declared Jews to be the "elder brothers" of the Christian faith. Recently Pope Francis said that inside every Christian is a Jew.

In line with this morning's three readings, let us listen to God's whispers in our hearts, cling to Christ during the storms of our lives, and be grateful that true life comes from Jesus, the Jewish Messiah given to the Jews for the sake of the entire world.

Homily 63

MARY MAGDALENE AT THE TOMB AND NEW CREATION

"I have seen the Lord"

THIS MORNING'S GOSPEL EVOKES the darkness and void in Genesis—the beginning—out of which God summons life and light. The first day. The sixth day: in the image of God he created them; male and female he created them. And it was very good. Creation. Chaos comes again. Judas goes into the dark to betray his Lord. Darkness descends on the little weeping group at the cross. And now, still in the darkness, the first day of the *new* week. *The new creation.* The eighth day. Women at the tomb; perhaps to bring more spices, perhaps just to weep, perhaps just to be there, because there was nowhere else to be. Nothing else to do. Nothing else that mattered.

Mary Magdalene does not feature in John's Gospel until her appearance with the other Marys at the foot of the cross. I emphasize that the Magdalene is neither Mary of Bethany nor the sinful woman who washed Jesus' feet with her tears. She is the one described as the one out of whom seven demons were driven. But Mary Magdalene's presence is spectacular. Mary weeps. Perhaps one only sees angels when one weeps. John's Gospel also evokes Cana where Jesus changed water into wine. They have taken away my master. The grief of love. The Song of Songs. The world's grief, Israel's grief, concentrated in Mary's grief. Echoes of the searching lover in the Song of Songs.

MARY MAGDALENE AT THE TOMB

The Emmaus disciples did not recognize Jesus. The disciples on the boat did not recognize Jesus; Mary Magdalene does not recognize Jesus either. He must be the gardener. The garden of Eden, the new Adam and the new Eve. He called his mother "Woman" both at Cana and on the cross. Now Jesus asks the Magdalene: "Woman, why are you weeping?"

Remember what Pilate said: "Behold the man." Here is the man: the new Adam, the seed of the new creation. The gardener, charged with bringing the chaos of God's creation into new order, into flower, into fruitfulness.

The Magdalene is the first apostle, the apostle to the apostles, the first to bring the Good News that the tomb was empty. A greater privilege yet: the first to see, to meet, to speak with the risen Master himself. This passage clearly states that something extraordinary has taken place. Not only with Jesus—though that is extraordinary enough—but to the way the world is, the way God is. Up to this point Jesus had spoken about God as his Father, or "my Father." He called his followers, disciples, servants, and friends. Now all that is changed.

He says to Mary Magdalene: "Go and say to my *brothers*: I'm going to my Father and *your* Father, to my God and *your* God. Something been decisively changed. The disciples are welcomed into a new world: they can know God the way Jesus knew God; they can be intimate children with the Father. They can be true Israelites at last. Israel's calling was to be God's son, God's firstborn. Until Jesus calls her name, she does not know him. He is the same; He is different. He is alive, filled with a new kind of life. Let the risen Jesus call your own name.

"Stop clinging to me." It is more likely that this was a warning to Mary that the new relationship with him was not going to be like the old one. He would not be going around Galilee and Judea anymore, walking the lanes with them, sharing meals, discussing, talking, praying. They would see him now and then but soon it will be a time for him to go to the Father. The gospel evoking pregnancy and giving birth, sorrow and then joy.

Mary is not upset by this. She has business at hand. Once again she is the apostle to the apostles. I have seen the master, Rabouni, and he called me Mary. "I have seen the Lord."

Homily 64

FEAST OF SAINTS PAUL AND PETER

"Simon son of John, do you love me more than these?"

WE COMMEMORATE THIS MORNING of the seventh Friday after Easter with readings about Sts. Paul and Peter, two pillars of the church who had denied Jesus but were transformed by their encounters with the risen Christ. Thereafter, both understood themselves, the church, and the cosmos in the light of the crucified and risen Christ. Let us pray this morning to deepen our crucifixion and resurrection world-view.

Many years ago around this time, I was ordained and said my First Mass. My sister asked me recently if I ever had any regrets becoming a priest. I have never looked back, and I lived during the turbulent mid-sixties and early seventies. What a great grace and joy it is to be a priest.

This morning's first reading centers on St. Paul and his difficulties with the Jewish and Roman authorities because the crucified and risen Christ was his Lord, not the Jewish Law and certainly not Caesar. Paul, a man who, as this reading says, viewed his own life of no importance as long as he could bear witness to what he calls "the gospel, the good news of God's grace." Notice what Paul says in Romans one: "Paul, a servant of Christ Jesus, called to be an apostle and set apart for the *gospel* of God—the *gospel* he promised beforehand through his prophets in the holy scriptures regarding his Son, who as to his earthly life was a descendant of David, and who through the spirit of holiness was appointed the son of God in power by his resurrection from the dead: Jesus Christ our Lord." This is the gospel and no other

FEAST OF SAINTS PAUL AND PETER

The only time in my life that I have been profoundly moved by relics is when I approached and prayed at St. Paul's tomb in the Church of Paul in Chains outside of the walls of Rome. Our faith is incarnational, rooted in Christ, the seed of the new creation. The flesh is the hinge of salvation and this is the reason why Catholics reverence relics.

Today's reading from John's Gospel centers on another resurrection appearance of Jesus to his disciples. The rich, homey details found in John contradict those who speak of his Gospel as the most "spiritual gospel." The disciples initially fail to recognize Jesus, a feature of most of the resurrection appearances. The Beloved Disciple's quick faith prompts him to confess, "it is the Lord." Impetuous Peter jumps in for a swim so that he can be with Jesus sooner than the others.

What does he find? Jesus on the beach cooking a meal of bread and fish over a charcoal fire. This evokes the fire at which Peter warmed himself when he denied his Lord three times. Two points: notice how Jesus does not scold or castigate Peter for his cowardly denial, or the other disciples for their spineless abandonment during Jesus' passion and death. Julian of Norwich wrote, *"for we do not fall in the sight of God, and we do not stand in our own sight."* Peter's rehabilitation and commissioning is fraught with loving irony: a threefold, "do you love me more than these?" And Peter's more than uncomfortable confession, "you know that I do." Then Jesus' "feed my lambs" commissions him as the under-shepherd to the chief shepherd mentioned in 1 Peter 5:1–4, and evokes the good shepherd willing to lay down his life for his sheep. Jesus also tells Peter, in essence, mind your own business, follow me, and never mind what will happen to the Beloved Disciple. You will, however, suffer when you too will be crucified.

The Jesuit superior general who is credited with rebuilding the Jesuits after the suppression, Johannes Roothaan, cautioned Jesuits against contemplating the resurrection too much because it would make them lax. I disagree strongly, however, with the former superior. Living the mysticism of everyday life means experiencing the cross *and resurrection* in our daily humdrum lives of aging, illness, the decline of vocations, the secularization of our institutions, the attacks on the church, and the brokenness both of ourselves and our culture.

Let us call upon the God and Father of our Lord Jesus Christ, the God who raised Jesus from the dead to instill in us a resurrection-faith courage, which flows from risen Jesus' Holy Spirit of Pentecost to renew the face of the earth.

Homily 65

PAUL: THE ECSTATIC MYSTIC

"When I am weak, then I am strong."

THE APOSTLE PAUL'S CONFESSION in this morning's first reading is strikingly paradoxical. Here is a man who had not only enjoyed an encounter with the risen Christ that made him an apostle but also a man in *Christ* who was taken up to the third heaven and into paradise. Paul is the symbol of the ecstatic mystic who had a foretaste of the beatific vision granted to us only after death. Yet—he emphasized that he was content with weakness, wanting to know only Christ and him *crucified*.

Although everyone here has had experiences in which one exclaims, "why can't life be like this all the time?"—I have fond memories of surfing among dolphins, dancing with an orangutan, being kissed by a killer whale, and nuzzling a domesticated Alaskan wolf—I suspect that we are more aware of how ordinary are lives are. Even the ecstatic mystic Paul, moreover, had to face the daily grind of being an apostle to the gentiles, often ridiculed and persecuted for preaching a crucified Messiah. "I am not ashamed of the gospel," he wrote. And on the surface it was something to be ashamed of: Jesus became *sin*; he who hangs upon a tree is *cursed*. Paul had to preach that a cursed man, made sin, was Israel's Messiah. His life was filled with hunger, thirst, and cold, shipwrecked a few times, beaten with rods, lashed several times, and finally in prison awaiting death by the sword because as a Roman citizen he could not be crucified. In a sense, nothing had changed: the Romans were still in charge; Herod was still the pseudoking; the Temple remained unfinished, and for most Jews, life went on as

PAUL: THE ECSTATIC MYSTIC

usual. But Paul knew that because of Christ crucified and risen, everything had changed.

Karl Rahner, the influential 20th century German Jesuit theologian, admitted being amazed and confused that Jesus' life was in some ways so ordinary, so banal, so daily grind. Unknown for thirty years, an itinerate preacher for three, even his crucifixion by the Romans was in some ways no different from what thousands had experienced from Roman hands. To be sure, his resurrection puts everything in a different light. For Rahner the first thing that we should learn from Jesus is to be fully human! If Jesus is the God-man, then he is God *in the everyday*. Within that context, Rahner wrote of a "mysticism of daily life." He stressed that our ordinary, banal, humdrum daily life is the stuff real Christianity where grace—God's presence—has its history and is *actually experienced there*.

The mystic of everyday life, for Rahner, is simply someone who can die to self and surrender to the Mystery who embraces his or her life—one who can accept with hope the experience of utter loneliness; who can forgive with no expectation of the other's gratitude or even of feeling good about one's selflessness; who prays, even when it feels useless; who maintains faith, hope, and love—even when there are no apparent reasons for so doing; who experiences bitterly the great gulf between what we desire from life and what it actually gives us; who courageously, totally accepts life and oneself even when everything that props up his or her fails. Wherever space is really left by forgetting oneself, by apparent emptiness, by the many mini-deaths of daily life—provided that emptiness is not filled by nonsense, busyness, or chatter, or the deadly grief of the world—there God is. Because of Christ, the mysticism of daily life is one of joy in the world and an Easter faith that loves the earth—but anchored in the cross. "When I am weak, then I am strong."

Homily 66

ST. FRANCIS OF ASSISI'S STIGMATA AND THE STIGMATA OF DAILY LIFE

"I bear on my body the marks of Jesus"

ST. FRANCIS OF ASSISI lived to the full what this morning's readings emphasize: finding true life in Christ's cross. Called the "seraphic" saint, the "angel of the sixth seal," a "second Moses," and even "another Christ," as a faithful mirror of Christ, "the little poor man," is undoubtedly the world's most popular saint, one admired and loved—and not only by Catholics. I suspect that he has become even more popular because of Pope Francis, who called him the saint closest to his heart.

This playboy, soldier, and lover of glory who was severely wounded and suffered from ill health underwent a profound conversion and became a mystic who progressed from a hermit-like existence to one more apostolic, to preaching, serving society's outcasts, and founding an order. He wrote: "When I was in sin, it was very bitter to me to see lepers. And the Lord himself brought me among them. What had seem bitter to me was changed to sweetness of body and soul. After this, I left the world." Francis wrote of an ecstasy that absorbed him in a light that enlarged his spirit through which he fell totally in love with the Trinity, with Jesus-Messiah crucified, and embraced radical poverty. Although never ordained, Francis had such a great love for the Eucharist that he and his followers reverenced the clergy, regardless of their sins and faults. He also emphasized preaching orthodox "safe doctrine" and possessed an experiential, loving, empathetic thinking with the hierarchical church. When Francis's doctors told him to

ST. FRANCIS OF ASSISI'S STIGMATA

cease weeping because of the damage it was doing to his eyes, he replied, "what are these that I have in common with flies?"

On September of 1244, the seraph-angel-crucified-Christ imprinted on Francis's body his sacred wounds—what Dante called "the final seal." Francis is now known as *the stigmatic*—the universal archetype of this sign of divine favor. St. John of the Cross wrote that sometimes the soul is so inflamed in love that the effects progress outward—even to the body—and are directly proportional to the strength of that love. That probably explains why my bypass surgeon said that my heart was the only one he had ever seen with 666 inscribed upon it.

There is also the stigmata of everyday life, of anonymous stigmatics who more or less bleed daily for Christ. They are faithful to the demands of daily life despite the suffering caused by hardship, disappointments, misunderstandings, difficult work, poor relationships, failure, illness, depression, or old age. Let us also ponder the ways in which we make each other bleed—whether intentionally or unintentionally. On this feast let us think of all those whose daily lives fill up what is lacking in Christ's sufferings—anonymous stigmatics—in order to plod away at awakening in those we serve a small spark of faith, of hope, and of love. "I bear on my body the marks of Jesus." With St. Ignatius, let us pray, "Jesus, within your wounds hide me."

Homily 67

FRANCIS OF ASSISI AND IGNATIUS LOYOLA

"I bear on my body the marks of Jesus."

ST. FRANCIS OF ASSISI lived to the full what this evening's readings emphasize: the cross, how all creation praises God, and intimately knowing Jesus and his Father. Francis has been called the "seraphic" saint, the "angel of the sixth seal," a "second Moses," and even "another Christ." As a faithful mirror of Christ, the *Poverello,* "the little poor man," is undoubtedly the world's most popular saint, one admired and loved—and not only by Catholics. I suspect that he has become even more popular because of Pope Francis.

In his interviews, however, Pope Francis mentions both Francis of Assisi and Ignatius of Loyola, so I wish now to emphasize how much they have in common—despite their differences. Both were playboys, soldiers who loved glory, were severely wounded, suffered from ill health, and underwent profound conversions. Both were mystics who progressed from a hermit-like existence to one more apostolic—to preaching, serving the poor and society's outcasts, and founding an order. Francis of Assisi wrote: "when I was in sin, it was very bitter to me to see lepers. And the Lord himself brought me among them. What had seemed bitter to me was changed to sweetness of body and soul. After this, I left the world."

Francis wrote of an ecstasy that absorbed him in a light that enlarged his spirit;, Ignatius, at the river Cardoner, of becoming a new man with a new understanding that comprehended matters of *both* faith and of

FRANCIS OF ASSISI AND IGNATIUS LOYOLA

learning. Clearly, Francis and Ignatius found God in *all* things. Both Francis and Ignatius fell totally in love with the Trinity and with Christ crucified—and embraced radical poverty. Ignatius had such a great reverence for the priesthood and Eucharist (his many mystical graces involved the Eucharist) that he postponed saying Mass for a year to prepare himself better to do so. Francis—although never ordained— had such great love for the Eucharist that he and his followers reverenced the clergy, regardless of their often glaring sins and faults.

Francis and Ignatius both emphasized preaching orthodox "safe doctrine" and an experiential, loving, empathetic thinking, with the hierarchical church. When Francis's doctors told him to cease weeping because of the damage it was doing to his eyes, he retorted, "what are these that I have in common with flies?" When doctors told Ignatius the same about his copious weeping, Ignatius stopped for the sake of the *apostolate*! And one need only glance at his *Spiritual Diary* to know how important tears were to Ignatius.

Ignatius prayed for Christ to hide him in his wounds. But on September of 1244, the seraph-angel-crucified-Christ imprinted on Francis's body his sacred wounds—what Dante called "the final seal." Francis is now known as *the stigmatic*—the universal archetype of this sign of divine favor. John of the cross wrote that sometimes the soul is so inflamed in love that the effects progress outward—even to the body—and are directly proportional to the strength of that love. This probably explains why the bypass surgeon said that my heart was the only one he had ever seen with 666 inscribed upon it.

I wish now to speak of the stigmata of everyday life, of the anonymous stigmatics whom I know, Jesuits who more or less bleed daily for Christ. Our superiors. Jesuits willing to get up at all hours to drive someone to the airport or hospital; the Boston College president, administrators, chairmen, professors, chaplains, and the like, who are daily being nibbled to death by pollywogs. Those in our community who work almost constantly with little time for themselves; those who do their university work, despite depression and/or illness. Those teaching and writing to obtain tenure—I would rather die for Christ than write for Christ. The foreign Jesuit graduate students—some struggling with culture shock, language, and do not know what awaits them when they return to their country. And—let us also ponder the ways in which we make each other bleed— whether intentionally or unintentionally.

In short, I think of all those Jesuits I know, whose daily lives fill up what is lacking in Christ's sufferings—anonymous stigmatics—in order to plod away at awakening in those we serve a small spark of faith, of hope, and of love. "I bear on my body the marks of Jesus." As St. Ignatius prayed, "Jesus, within your wounds hide me."

Homily 68

THE FEAST OF IGNATIUS OF LOYOLA

"Whoever does not carry his own cross and come after me cannot be my disciple."

WHEN A SENIOR AT Worcester Polytechnic Institute, I read an article in the *Saturday Evening Post* entitled, "The Jesuits: the Pope's Commandos." Despite the article's sensationalism and half-truths, the author made one observation that resonated deeply with me. Ignatius and his companions were not only men obsessed with serving God and his church, but they also considered the entire world as their kneeler. In their praise and service of God, they found God in *all* things.

Knowing that I wanted to be one of the pope's commandos, (I now prefer the term "navy seal"), I left my electrical engineering position at Boeing in Seattle, and entered the Society of Jesus. When Jorge Mario Bergoglio became the two-hundred-sixty-sixth and first Jesuit Pope in 2013, it *pleased* me that he took the name *Francis* and *not* Ignatius. Why? Because, even today, the name Ignatius of Loyola is controversial. Unlike St. Francis of Assisi, Ignatius's name evokes either love or hate, rarely neutrality or indifference. Even within the church that canonized him, some find it difficult to mention his name and regard him with suspicion. Nonetheless, he commands awe and respect, if only grudgingly given at times, from most who know anything at all about his extraordinary accomplishments.

Ignatius began his "worldly" career as a courtier, a gentleman, and a quasi-soldier who loved honor, glory, dueling, women, and gambling. After a profound religious conversion initiated by a severe battle injury, he became a wandering pilgrim, a harsh ascetic for the sake of Christ, and attained heroic sanctity. He decided to study for the priesthood so that he could better help people spiritually. He gathered a group of companions in Christ, founded a renowned religious order, established colleges, charitable institutions, and always kept his hand in directly pastoral activity. He directed a vast missionary network, and undertook sensitive diplomatic appointments. Moreover, he authored the highly influential *Spiritual Exercises*, the Jesuit *Constitutions* (upon which numerous religious orders are founded), and thousands of letters that demonstrate his far reaching sociopolitical involvement.

When in conversation with a retired Benedictine priest, he asked me how I could possibly be writing a book on Ignatius *the mystic*. Ignatius's apostolic successes and those of his men have overshadowed for many his mystical prowess. Ignatius of Loyola, however, is one of the Christian tradition's profoundest mystics and perhaps its greatest mystagogue, that is, one who leads others into the deepest mystery of the Trinity, the crucified and risen Jesus Christ—and into one's own mystery as a human being. His *Spiritual Diary* had been judged to be one of the purest examples of direct reporting of mystical experiences in Christian history.

In short, Ignatius was immediately and directly conscious of the presence of the triune God, Christ, and Mary—present in the way that lovers are present to each other. He understood how God had created the world, how our Lord Jesus Christ was present in the Eucharist—my favorite, at the consecration during Mass, the virgin Mary showed him that her own flesh was in that of her Son. Ignatius did not stress mystical experiences and mystical states for their own sake, however, but as a means to *seek, find, and accomplish God's will.*

Ignatius made the extraordinary claim that his *Spiritual Exercises* would enable a person to seek and to find God's specific will for him or her. He asserted that "the creator and Lord" *himself* would "deal directly" with the person by inflaming him or her with love and "dispose him [or her] for the better service of God and neighbor in the future." Ignatius's mysticism is primarily one that seeks, finds, and carries out God's will. In addition, this love-consciousness of the triune God, the God-man, Mary—and numerous secondary mystical phenomena expressed themselves in *service* to the poor, the orphaned, the sick, and the uneducated—from whom Ignatius was never far.

THE FEAST OF IGNATIUS OF LOYOLA

To be with the trinitarian Christ to serve his church may well be a good short formula of Ignatius's spirituality and mysticism. Another can be found in his "contemplation to obtain divine love," in which he asks for interior knowledge of all the great blessings he has received, in order that, stirred to profound *gratitude*, he may be able to *love and serve* the divine majesty in all things."

On this feast of St. Ignatius let us ask ourselves questions dear to Ignatius's heart: "What have I done for Christ? What am I doing for Christ? What will I do for Christ? And pray with the words that concluded Ignatius's thousands of letters: *May God grant us abundant grace to know his most holy will and perfectly to fulfill it.*

Homily 69

FEAST OF TERESA OF AVILA

"She who abides in me, and I in her, she it is who bears much fruit."

S T. TERESA OF AVILA lived to the full what today's Mass readings emphasize: Spirit-filled prayer, Spirit and life from God's word, and abiding in Christ. Teresa of Avila is perhaps the greatest woman mystic in the Christian tradition and was gifted with an extraordinary ability to describe even the highest stages of mystical prayer. You cannot read a better book on prayer than her *Autobiography* in which she defines prayer "as nothing else than an intimate sharing between friends and taking time frequently to be alone with him whom we know loves us."

Teresa insisted that her eminent learning came directly from God. She wrote, "my soul suddenly found itself *learned*. The mystery of the most holy Trinity, together with other lofty things, was so clearly explained to me that there is no theologian with whom I would not have the boldness to contend in defense of the truth of these marvels." We have been baptized in the name of the Father, Son, and Holy Spirit. The Trinity dwells within us. Let us pray, therefore, with St. Teresa, not to a vague *God* but to the *God and Father* of our Lord Jesus Christ, to his crucified and risen Son, and to the Holy Spirit of their love.

Teresa of Avila is also known for her use of striking images. For example, she likened the soul to a silkworm. "When full-grown," she wrote, "it starts to spin its silk and to build the house in which it is to die. This house may be understood to mean Christ. When the soul is truly dead to the world, a little white butterfly comes forth." In her masterpiece, *The*

Interior Castle, Teresa describes the human soul as an extremely beautiful diamond castle that contains many rooms, paralleling the many heavenly mansions. God himself dwells in the center of this castle and continually invites the person to come inside to remain in his truth and love. Prayer is the way one enters.

From her numerous and varied mystical experiences, I'll focus on the one immortalized in Bernini's famous statue, "the Ecstasy of St. Teresa." Teresa wrote: "I saw a small, very beautiful angel in bodily form beside me—his face blazing with light. I saw in his hands a long dart of gold, with fire at the end. He thrust it through my heart several times. It caused me to burn with a great love of God and left me satisfied with God alone."

In matters concerning the reforming of the Carmelite order—which she undertook with St. John of the Cross—Teresa showed herself to be shrewd and pragmatic. I appreciate the way she treated her nuns. A firm but pragmatic woman with a subtle sense of ecclesiastical and secular politics, she showed herself to be quite capable of outmaneuvering bishops and secular authorities—*when* God's will indicated a certain line of action.

I marvel at my favorite woman saint who made no bones about enjoying a good meal with good wine—but always left some wine in the glass as a small penance for her failings. When a nun showed me her cell at Avila, I remarked how small it was. The nun said, "well, she wasn't home much."

On September 27, 1970, Pope Paul VI solemnly declared Teresa of Avila a doctor of the church—a title she and St. Catherine of Siena were simultaneously the first women to bear. In 1997, Pope John Paul II declared St. Thérèse of Lisieux a doctor of the church and in October of last year, Pope Benedict conferred the honor upon St. Hildegard of Bingen. I recommend the movie, *Vision,* an extraordinary portrayal of Hildegard. To become a doctor of the church, a person must possess notable sanctity, distinguished learning, and be proclaimed doctor by either a pope or an ecumenical council. Because this title is associated with the church's own teaching office and had been bestowed only upon men, some theologians assumed that a woman could not hold the title. So, on this occasion, let us praise God for the incredible good wrought in the church by women. I've read many of the women mystics—and with great profit. I was taught by nuns and will be grateful to them until the day I die. "She who abides in me, and I in her, she it is who bears much fruit."

Homily 70

FEAST OF THE HOLY ANGELS

"Lord, in the sight of the angels I will sing your praises."

You know Dasher, Dancer, Prancer, and Vixen; Comet, Cupid, Donner, and Blitzen. But do you recall the most famous reindeer of all? Rudolph the red nose reindeer! Also, people my age and even younger can easily name Snow White's seven dwarfs: Bashful, Doc, Dopey, Grumpy, Happy, Sleepy, and Sneezy.

Now—can you name the archangels? Michael, Gabriel, Raphael—and poor Uriel usually gets left out. In my youth, the Mass preface listed the seven choirs of angels: seraphim, cherubim, thrones, dominions, virtues, powers, principalities, archangels, and angels. But for good measure, let us not forget our personal guardian angels.

I take angels seriously because of their frequency in Scripture, tradition, and the liturgy. I'm personally quite attracted to the gospel scenes in which the angel Gabriel tells Mary that she will give birth to the savior (how moved I was when my eyes fell on Fra Angelico's famous Annunciation painting in Florence), the angel who warns Joseph about impending harm to Jesus, the angel who ministered to Jesus after his testing by Satan in the desert, and the angel who strengthened Jesus during his agony in the garden.

I am also especially fond of Jesus instructing his disciples not to despise children because their angels always see the face of his heavenly Father. And as a Jesuit, I appreciate Ignatius of Loyola's frequent admonition to contemplate how I am standing before God our Lord, and of his *angels,* and of the saints interceding for me. That said, as an aside, I enjoy the comic strip "Rose is a Rose," that sometimes focuses on the child Pasquale and his intriguing guardian angel. And, on my grammar school classroom seat I made room for my guardian angel.

Of course, there is something to the complaint that our age makes it difficult to believe in the triune God, the God-man Jesus, let alone angels. Nevertheless, I have long been fascinated by the church's emphasis on our *social* nature, that life here and the afterlife comprise our relationships not only with God, but also with the entire communion of saints, *angels* included, and all creation, animals, vegetation, insects, rivers, oceans, mountains, etc. All creation praises and will praise God. Moreover, if science has made it highly likely that life exists on other planets, I find belief in the existence of angels more than plausible. When one Jesuit challenged my belief in and devotion to angels, I asked him if he said the Mass of the Holy Angels, of the Guardian Angels, and noticed how often angels appear in the overall liturgy? The law of prayer is the law of belief. Sounds better in Latin: Lex orandi; lex credendi.

The exterior of Boston's College's lovely gothic old library has ten angelic representations. The exterior of the exquisite gothic building in which I live features twenty-seven angels. Our magnificent chapel has sixty-two angels, some of remarkable artistic beauty. The rotunda in another splendid building, Gasson Hall, contains an imposing statue of Michael the archangel stepping on Satan's head. When asked about the statue, I tell people that Michael is stepping on a Jesuit's head. The representations point beyond themselves to the spiritual beings who are a sign of the mysterious wonder and holiness of God whom they praise without ceasing and of a creation far more mysterious than our overly materialistic world considers it to be.

Belief in angels came to permeate medieval Christian society as deeply as belief in evolution steeps ours. How ironic: the contemporary mind focuses on apes to understand human nature; the medieval mind, on seraphic and cherubic angels. Medieval theology enabled the shift from the monastic to the scholastic view of angels. The monks saw themselves in terms of the angels and studied them to lead a deeper spiritual life. That the angels strengthen Christians in time of trial, illuminate their minds, and inflame their wills seems to correspond to the threefold mystical path of purgation, illumination, and union. The angelic hierarchies did provide some of the language and concepts used for expressing the mystics' often intense and unmediated experiences of God. The Scholastic theologians also linked their speculations to the spiritual needs of the faithful, but did so with great theological precision and subtlety. For them, the angels are Stoics in affection (except during the crucifixion), Aristotelians in epistemology and metaphysics, and Neoplatonists in their hierarchy of being and illumination.

One must not overlook the social-political consequences of angelology. Because of the atemporal, hierarchic nature of the angels, they became the ideal models of the stability and harmony that should exist in society, religious orders, the church, and the state. If Scripture teaches that the church is to judge the angels and that angels are above secular rulers, then the church is above secular rulers and can judge them. Thus, a belief in angels at one time had serious political consequences.

The historical role of the angels—especially of those found in the Book of Revelation—sometimes laid the ground for revolutionary ecclesiastical movements and even military activity. The Franciscans understood both St. Francis of Assisi and themselves in terms of the angels. This led them to ask if they were to lead the church into Joachim of Fiore's age of the Holy Spirit, into the age of seraphic contemplation, into an age of a transformed or even a replaced church.

The cult of the warrior-saint Michael helped to Christianize the crusades and played a prominent role in the often violent conversion of the Nordic people. Moreover, as emphasis shifted from Michael the archangel to the Virgin Mary, social values became more important than military ones. Theology and its concomitant practices do have consequences.

When confronted with the often sarcastic derision of those who ask me how many angels can dance on the head of a pin, I reply: it depends on whether they are dancing cheek to cheek, square dancing, doing ballet, or dancing the hokey pokey. Do contemporary scientist face similar ridicule for figuring out to the billionth of a millimeter every movement and position in the *dance of* the electrons? Have you ever asked: "How many people's *thoughts* can be concentrated upon the head of a pin?" In any case, the medieval question was mostly a debating exercise or a word game in much the same way that the BBC's excellent *My Word* program would take a well-known sentence and transform it into something rather amusing. I remember an issue of a serious philosophical journal not many years ago that was dedicated to the question: "Does it rain between the drops?"

I conclude with one of the divine praises, praises I often pray; "blessed be God in *his angels* and in his saints."

Homily 71

THE FEAST OF MARTYRS AND JESUS' PRESENCE AND ABSENCE

"Now is your time of grief, but I will see you again and no one will take away your joy."

WE COMMEMORATE TODAY THE martyrdom of Charles Lwanga and his companions. The third-century church father, Tertullian, wrote that the blood of martyrs is the seed of the church. The contemporary African church is growing by leaps and bounds. One indication: the number of African Jesuits who studied and are now studying at Boston College.

Martyrdom is the most dramatic way of imitating Christ crucified and giving witness to the Christian faith. Would you give your life for Christ? Would I? I would hope so, but there are days when I think that if someone said, "your faith or your Mac computer," I might hesitate.

This morning's gospel—with its emphasis on grief and joy—evokes the Song of Songs and its focus on the absence and presence of the beloved and the concomitant grief and joy this causes. The twelfth-century mystical theologian, Richard of St. Victor, wrote about the Trinity: "But if nothing is more present than the absent one, if nothing is more absent than the most present one, is anything more marvelous, anything more incomprehensible? God's absence and presence—grief and joy—God's spiritual peek-a-boo with us. I have vivid memories of my sister hiding briefly from her baby and how he would cry and then burst into laughter when she showed herself. Human peek-a-boo. I used to take my sister's family dog for long walks in the woods and allowed him to roam. But if I hid myself, he would become quite agitated. When I showed myself, he would get on with his frolicking. More human peek-a-boo.

Of course the context of this grief-joy, absence-presence in John's Gospel refers to Jesus' horrifying death, which will take him away from and grieve his disciples. Then, his consoling resurrection appearances: presence and joy. "Peace be with you." They could not believe it for joy!!!

When studying in Germany, I heard more than one story about women after the war waiting for the arrival of the troop train, which carried back the surviving German soldiers. One can only imagine the joy of seeing one's loved one alive—and the grief because of the absent loved one.

To be sure, John's Gospel highlights another facet of Jesus' life, death, resurrection, and ascension. Mary Magdalene grieves at Jesus' tomb. He appears and she grabs his feet. "Stop clinging to me," Jesus says, "I have not yet ascended to the Father." Jesus is telling Mary and us that his permanent presence is not by way of his bodily appearances but as the exalted Lord of heaven and earth. Paul wrote, "last of all he appeared to me," but, as we heard yesterday, Jesus says: "I shall be with you always." "Blessed are those who have not seen, but believe."

Which of us here has not experienced in prayer, at the roots of our being, and in our daily lives both the painful absence and joyful presence of the Lord.? St. Ignatius of Loyola—as well as many other saints—wrote of the Holy Spirit bestowing courage, strength, consolation, tears, inspirations, and peace—palpable signs of the Lord's presence. The evil spirit makes us tepid, sad, disquiet, heavy. The grief from absence.

St. Catherine of Genoa wrote: "If one drop of what my heart is feeling were to fall into hell, hell itself would become heaven itself." When I feel the Lord's presence, I can take on the world, the flesh, and the devil. When he seems absent, I want my mommy. We have been baptized into the death and resurrection of Jesus Christ. Why should we not therefore expect absence and presence, grief and joy—the mysticism of daily life, the mysticism of daily death—and how often that occurs in small ways—and the mysticism of daily resurrection—again in small ways.

St. Ignatius did not focus on feelings but on being with Christ to serve—on seeking, finding, and carrying out God's will. The letters of Mother Teresa make crystal clear that she faithfully served Christ, despite her more than fifty years of frightful mystical dereliction. Even with this long and profound spiritual void, she could pray before the crucifix at the end of her life: "Lord, I have never denied you anything."

Homily 72

MOTHER TERESA: WRESTLING WITH GOD

"You shall be called Israel, one who wrestled with God."

I RECEIVED AN EMAIL years ago from a German friend. We both studied under Karl Rahner in Germany in the early seventies. He left the Jesuits, married, and I've known the wife for over forty years. Years ago they found their eldest son hanging from a tree and ten years ago their youngest son was killed in an automobile accident. What tragedy! He, his wife, and the remaining son are trying to make sense of it all. Wrestling with God's mysterious ways.

Mother Teresa, called the "saint of the gutters" and "the saint of God's thirst to love and be loved by humanity," is appreciated primarily for her service to the poorest of the poor. Her extraordinary mystical depths, however, came to light only a few years ago because of the publication of her private correspondence. Early in her life as a nun, Mother Teresa took an exceptional private vow to consider even the smallest voluntary refusal to submit to God's will to be a "mortal sin." This private vow was the motivation behind all she did and one of "her greatest secrets."

Mother Teresa's writings contain only a brief statement about the one-year long honeymoon period during which she mystically experienced so much of God's loving presence. Soon afterwards, spiritual darkness, interior suffering, deep loneliness, acute feelings of emptiness, and of her own nothingness consumed her inner life. Her feelings of love for God, for Christ, and for others—as well as any experience of faith, hope, and love—simply vanished. The bone-marrow excruciation of God's absence, of God's rejection, of fear that her soul, Jesus, and heaven were illusions, and—paradoxically—of a radical longing for God became her inner hell for more than half a century. She prayed on more than one occasion: "God, what are you doing to one so small?" Shortly before her death, she was heard praying to Christ crucified: "I have never refused you anything. You are hard." "It often happens," she wrote, "that those who spend their time giving light to others, remain in darkness themselves. If I ever become a saint—I will surely be one of darkness. I will continually be absent from heaven—to light the light of those in darkness on earth." She who wrestled with God.

On the other hand, the third order Franciscan mystic, Blessed Angela of Foligno, claimed to have experienced in this life some form of the beatific vision. She wrote of a divine working in her soul that was "so deep and ineffable an abyss that this presence of God alone is the good that the saints enjoy in eternal life." On three separate occasions Angela found herself in a most exalted and ineffable way "standing or lying in the Trinity" and saw the "all Good" in darkness. When the Trinity plunged her into his "extremely deep abyss," it removed all fear from her soul and secured it firmly in faith and hope. Incapable of describing this experience, she cried out, "whatever I say about it is blasphemy." She who wrestles with God.

Not only we Christians wrestle with God—with all the ups and downs that entails. The Jewish patriarch Jacob found out that God does not always play by our rules. I love the line: "When God saw that he could not prevail over Jacob, he struck his hip at its socket." I would have given God a red card. Also, I would go so far as to say that every person—believer, Hindu, Buddhist, Muslim, atheist, agnostic—wrestles with God because, sooner or later, everyone must wrestle with the depths of who and what we are. What matters is not the joys or the sorrows but being faithful to the crucifixion of daily life for our good and the good of others. In this way, a Christian, a non-Christian, an agnostic, an atheist does God's will and is faithful to his or her calling. We who wrestle with God!

HOMILIES FOR FAMILY OCCASIONS

Homily 73

A HOMILY FOR BAPTISM

"Let the little children come to me"

I AM FATHER HARVEY Egan and I welcome you to our baptism of Rumpelstiltskin. I've known his parents, Hensel and Gretel since 1965. I was honored to do your wedding, Hensel and Gretel. Given Rumpelstiltskin somewhat bumpy landing into this world, I am especially pleased to be here. A child is one of God's most precious gifts to a couple.

The first Christians viewed baptism principally as an adult initiation rite that led to table fellowship with Christ, that is, Mass with the reception of communion. As Christianity spread, however, entire households were baptized, indicating that the infants of converts were also baptized. And we celebrate today that infants are also invited to become Christians. Jesus said, "Let the children come to me." The Russian and Greek Orthodox go even further. The baby is baptized, confirmed, and given Eucharist—all at the same liturgy.

In some parts of the world people celebrate not only their birthdays but also their name day, their baptismal day on which they became Christians. Do you know the date of your baptism? When some of the great saints sinned, they would immediately recall their baptism and wash their souls in the primordial waters of baptism. When I was growing up, baptism was almost an exorcism rite that viewed the unbaptized baby as infected with Adam's sin and in the devil's power. The new rite, however, implies that even before baptism, *everyone* is called to be a beloved child of God for whom Christ died and rose bodily from the dead. Even before baptism,

God's love in Christ embraces every single person who comes into this world—and not only Christians.

Then why baptize this child? To express and make visible in the *church of Christ* that God is love and that Christ died and was raised for all. Through baptism, Rumpelstiltskin becomes a child of the church of Jesus Christ. No matter what he does with his life, he will never be able to change the fact that now the church is his mother, that God is his Father, that the crucified and risen Christ is his brother, and that he is loved and protected by the saints in heaven, the church on earth, and the church to come.

This two-thousand-year-old church is a world church, the *one church* founded by, won by, and united with Christ and his Holy Spirit—a world church in Asia, Africa, North and South America, Europe, and Australia to which he will now belong. Because of baptism, Rumpelstiltskin is now a child of eternity, one who will eventually be raised from the dead. He is now called to accept throughout his life his calling to be a disciple of the crucified and risen Christ. Rumpelstiltskin's life must give witness to this.

Before we baptize Rumpelstiltskin into this two-thousand-year-old church of Jesus Christ, remember that *you, your Christian faith, hope, and love*—as parents, godparents, grandparents, great grandparents, relatives, and friends—are the first church in which Rumpelstiltskin will grow. Please keep in mind that I am *not* the only one baptizing Rumpelstiltskin today. The *entire* church in Christ through me baptizes him. You as the church also baptize Rumpelstiltskin into Christ's life, death, and resurrection *and into your own faith*. You and I make him a disciple of the crucified and risen Christ. Please remember, also, that Christians have been doing this for two-thousand years! So, as we proceed with the rite of baptism, listen and look carefully, because everything done here pertains as much to you and to me as they do to Rumpelstiltskin. Let us also renew and deepen our appreciation for our own baptism, which we received years ago.

Homily 74

A MARRIAGE HOMILY

"This is why a man leaves his father and mother and cleaves to his wife, and they become one flesh."

Brad and Angelina, in a few moments you will pronounce your marriage vows. You will give your word of love and fidelity, which will radically change your lives. Before your family and friends gathered here as the church of Jesus Christ, you will give yourselves to each other totally and without reservations by making public, permanent, and holy the love you have for each other that has been growing for some time and will continue to grow.

Brad and Angelina, you are about to gather up and to give the mystery of your very own person in such a way that it can never be taken back. The most precious thing we have to give another person is our very self, our own uniqueness, our own mystery. The secret of marriage—the secret of life itself—is that you must give yourself.

An old English marriage vow formula dared to say, "with this ring, I thee adore!" We worship when we give our unique self totally to the mystery of another person—and never take it back. Love is never perfect in this life. Both of you are not marrying a saint. You are marrying, moreover, someone you will never fully know in this life, someone whose mystery and uniqueness you must respect because your names, Brad and Angelina, are written in God's hand. And love fills up the many cracks in daily life. The English saint, Thomas More, who gave his life rather than go back on his word, said, "when you give your word, you give yourself. Like water cupped into your hands, if you break your word, you break yourself like water flowing from uncupped hands."

Years ago I became friends with a young couple about to be married. I was stunned when they told me how annoyed they were that their parents, families, and friends wanted to attend their wedding. They considered their love to be so *private* that it belonged to them alone. They also made it clear that they wanted no children. I thought their love was only a selfishness for two.

In some countries the main person at a wedding is not the bride or the groom, but a masked and costumed person who never reveals his identity. He symbolizes that the bride and the groom are not really marrying each other, but are *being* married—not in a selfishness for two—but in the great process of human life that is much greater than any two people.

Please remember, too, that the self you are about to vow to each other is not entirely your own making. How much of the person you consider yourself to be is made up of the unselfish love given you by your mother and father, your sisters and brothers, your grandfathers and grandmothers, your relatives, and your friends? How quickly we forget the long history of family trees from which we come.

Over the years I have had the honor of baptizing babies at which the parents, grandparents, and even great-grand-parents were present. In order to be born, you needed: two parents, four grandparents, eight great-grandparents, sixteen great-great-grandparents, sixty-five fourth great grandparents, one-hundred-twenty-eight fifth great grandparents, two-hundred-fifty-six six great-grandparents, five-hundred-twelve seventh great grandparent, one-thousand-twenty-four eight great grandparents, and two-thousand-forty-eight ninth grade grandparents. For you to be born today from twelve previous generations, you needed a total of four-thousand-ninety-four ancestors over the last five-hundred years. Think for a moment—how many struggles? How many battles? How many difficulties? How much sadness? How much happiness? How many love stories? How many expressions of hope for the future did your ancestors have to undergo for you to exist at this present moment. The chain of life, and a clear symbol of how every marriage has a generational effect, a ripple effect, that goes beyond husband and wife.

You love each other now because you have *already* been loved by so many people, a chain of love with such a long history. And as one theologian wrote, "the pierced heart of Jesus Christ, who allowed himself sacrificially

A MARRIAGE HOMILY

to sink into death's infinite darkness upon the altar of the cross for his bride, the church. In this way he entrusted his spirit into his Father's hands—this is the source of the grace of sacramental marriage, which witnesses to Christ's grace by making public and explicit one's commitment of love."

Your family and friends could love and so can you only because the triune God through Christ crucified and risen first loved them and only because so many people before had loved them. Marriage is the only social institution in the Jewish scriptures expressly grounded in God's creative will. Man and woman, created in God's image and likeness, are two equally valuable complimentary manifestations of the one human reality. Behind this couple, there is always the One who embraces, preserves, redeems, and blesses all: the triune God, their silent partner. The triune God alone is the assurance of eternal *love*, grace, that ultimately is the only gift capable of filling human emptiness and meaninglessness.

Dwell in that love. Respect it. Respect each other. Sacrifice for each other. Never punish one another. Let respect and forgiveness always have the last word. Love one another more than yesterday, but less than tomorrow. Then the love and friendship you share will grow and deepen. If you suffer for each other, rejoice with each other, respect each other, live for each other, forgive each other, will you will remain friends, through thick and thin.

Many years ago, when I was anointing an old sea captain, his wife for over fifty years said to him: "Thank you for being such a good husband and father. Thank you for our children and grandchildren, for the life we shared together. Goodbye *friend*." My mother, married over fifty years, widowed for seventeen, told me almost every time I visited, "how I miss *my friend*."

Aelred of Rievaulx, the author of the marvelous fourteenth-century classic, *On Spiritual Friendship*, wrote: "God is friendship!" He calls the friendless person a "beast." Christ said to his disciples that he no longer called them servants, but *friends*. In a recent film, an angry husband shouted at his wife: "How is it that you are so gentle and friendly with strangers?" She replied: "Strangers are easy. The ones I'm supposed to love are the most difficult." How often the really small things of life destroy love and friendship.

Despite the very pious and churchy words you are hearing (and you will be hearing more), daily life, married or otherwise, is often as ordinary as hamburgers for lunch or stockings drying in the shower. But Christ himself lived this ordinary life to reveal how incredibly deep, important, and holy our lives should be—are! His life, death, and resurrection tell us that God is in love with us, that we are all secretly in love with each other, that God does care for us, and that our lives do have meaning. We are *all* made to receive and to give unconditional, daily, humdrum love—day in and day out, and this takes a lifetime.

Brad and Angelina, what all of us here today see is this secret love we all have for each other in Christ made visible in you. We see *in you* the mystery and the promise that human love in Christ holds out. A mystery, because you can love, we can love, unconditionally— only because Christ first loved us unconditionally. A promise, because only in heaven, shall we all belong to each other in perfect life and love. Brad and Angelina, this is what you mean to us today.

Homily 75

A FUNERAL HOMILY

"I am the resurrection and the life."

WHEN AGATHA CHRISTIE, THE famous mystery writer, was a young girl, her father died. Her relatives picked her to comfort her mother. She wrote: "I went timidly up to mother and touched her. 'Mummy, father is at peace now in heaven. He is happy. You wouldn't want him back, would you?' Suddenly my mother reared up in bed, with a sudden gesture that startled me into jumping back. 'Yes, I would,' she cried in a low voice. 'Yes, I would, I would do anything in the world to have him back, if I could. I want him, I want him back here, now, in this world with me.'"

When I was studying in Germany many years ago, Father Karl Rahner told me about a woman he knew who had two young sons who were about to be sent to the war on the Russian front. That meant almost certain death for her sons. The woman shouted at God and told God that he could not have her sons—how angry she was that God would even consider taking them. But they were sent to the front anyway and were killed. It astonished Rahner that a short time later this woman forgave God and she made her peace with God and herself.

It is very human to resent it when someone we love is taken from us. There is nothing wrong with feeling pain and even anger toward God. Even Jesus cried over the death of his friend Lazarus, but he did restore Lazarus's life. Even Jesus at one point in his life so feared death that his sweat was like blood. Even Jesus on the cross tasted the bitterness of death and cried out, "my God, my God, why have you forsaken me." Yet, Jesus so trusted his Father that even on the cross, he could say at the end: "Father, into your hands, I commend my spirit." And to prove that we can trust, yes trust, that God is our eternal life, our healing, and our comfort, Jesus' Father raised Jesus from the dead. So, if we are really Christians—not merely in name—we must see—sooner or later—God's loving hand in all that happens—even in death.

Again, we grieve for Walter Disney, but with a hope filled with faith in the risen Christ. Do you believe this? It is very hard to be a believing Christian in a country that does everything to deny the reality of death and proclaims in so many ways that there is nothing beyond this life. Which do you believe: our American culture with its denial of death and anything after death or the risen Christ who promises eternal life? Christianity is really as simple as believing that God has the last word and that word is life, life eternal.

The Bible says that if a person lives to be sixty, has a good spouse, sees his children and grandchildren grow up, has a good family and friends and some of the good things of life, ages with grace, and dies quickly and painlessly, then that person has been greatly blessed by God. Walter Disney was so blessed; he had a *full* life. let us remember that. CHILDREN'S NAMES you were blessed, too, by having a father, a father-in-law, a grandfather that really loved you. He lived for you, his family. You were the center of his life and what gave his life the most meaning.

GOOD PLACE TO INSERT A FEW FAMILY OR PERSONAL MEMORIES

I would not be here if I honestly did not believe that Walter Disney now lives a new, fulfilled, beautiful life in God. Now he not only sees God, but he also sees himself as the beautiful person he has become through his full life filled with God's loving care. He is now not only with God, but he is also with us in an even deeper way. The deeper anyone enters into God's life, the deeper he enters into the lives of all those whom God loves.

In many small towns in southern Germany, the cemetery is right outside the church. You cannot go into or leave church without passing through the cemetery. After a baptism, First Communion, Confirmation, or a wedding, the people go out of the church and introduce the newly baptized, confirmed, first communicant, or newlyweds to their buried loved ones right outside the church. Because of their deep faith, they know that their loved ones are still with them in the communion of saints, because they live in God. Do you want to feel Walter Disney's presence now? He is

A FUNERAL HOMILY

in Christ. Speak with him anytime, but especially when you receive Holy Communion. All this is the reason good Pope John XXIII could say, "every day is a good day to be born; every day is a good day to die." Let us not only pray for Walter Disney. Also pray to him because right now he is praying for us. *Saints of God, come to his aid! Hasten to meet him, angels of the Lord! Receive his soul and present him to God the Most High. Eternal rest grant unto him, O Lord, And let perpetual light shine upon him. May Walter now rest in peace. Amen.*

Homily 76

EULOGY FOR A BEST FRIEND

"Since God so loved us, we also ought to love one another."

STRENGTHENED BY THE CHURCH'S sacrament and accompanied by the prayers of his Jesuit brothers, his family, and friends, Father Michael A. Fahey died peacefully in the risen Lord at 2 in the afternoon, Friday, March 12th here at the Campion Health Center. He had loved his family, his friends, the church, his Jesuit brothers, his priestly vocation—and spent himself in their service."

Good morning. I'm Father Harvey Egan who has had the privilege of knowing the great Michael since 1966. We were next door neighbors for almost ten years. We shared many meals, conversations, and the splendid oysters at Legal Sea Foods, a special monthly treat for us. I find it instructive that Michael e-mailed me the day before he died. I happened to be re-reading a section in St. Augustine's *Confessions* in which he described his turmoil caused by the death of his close friend. So I'm pleased to be here to say something about my very best Jesuit friend in the crucified and risen Christ.

The Bible says that if a person lives to be sixty, has a good family and friends, some of the good things of life, ages with grace, and dies quickly and painlessly, then that person has been greatly blessed by God. Michael had much of that—but certainly not all. He did, however, have a full life. Eighty-seven years young; a Jesuit for almost seventy years; a priest for almost fifty-seven years. A *distinguished* career, fluent in French and German from his European studies, professor in several theological faculties, both in the United States and in Canada, a dean of theology, a superb teacher and outstanding dissertation director, editor of *Theological Studies*, a scholar's scholar, and an excellent pastor. He was also an accomplished chef and a great traveler who had even been to Moosup. There is a good Australian film, *My Brilliant Career*, and this applies to Michael.

Do we *mourn* Michael's passing to eternal life? Or course! In the edited words of Karl Rahner: "There is no substitute for Michael; there are no others who can fill the vacancy when one of those whom we have really loved, departs and is no longer with us. In true love, *no one replaces another*, for true love loves the *other person* in that depth where he is uniquely and irreplaceably himself. And thus, as death has trodden roughly through our lives, every one of the departed has taken a piece of our heart with him and often enough the whole heart." We grieve as *Christians*, however, filled with the hope we have from the *risen* Christ. I fully expect that Michael and I will meet again at Sts. Peter and Paul's new creation oyster bar.

Do we mourn Michael's passing to eternal life? No. We know just how much he *suffered* for many years—almost losing a foot and then the jaw cancer and the following complications. Almost the last thing he told me was that he had not eaten solid foods for over a year and that now even swallowing liquids was painful. Michael, however, *never complained* or wallowed in self-pity. We also do *not* mourn because we really believe that Michael at this time lives a new, fulfilled, beautiful life in God. Now he not only sees God, but he also sees *himself* as the beautiful person he has become through his full life filled with God's loving grace. He is now not only with God, but he is also *with us* in an even deeper way. The deeper anyone enters into God's life, the deeper one enters into the lives of all those whom God loves. That's why I know that Michael was aware of John and Meg's visit the evening before he died and the visit of his five nieces shortly after he had died. (You know that you are loved when you have nieces.)

When I ponder Michael's Jesuit life and his priestly bearing to the very day he died, what comes to mind is father Karl Rahner's stirring article, "Why Become or Remain a Jesuit?," in which he wrote: "I still see around me living in many of my companions a readiness for *selfless* service carried out in silence, for abandonment to God's incomprehensibility, for the calm acceptance of death in whatever form it may come, for total dedication to the following of Christ crucified." To be with Christ to serve is sometimes cited as a summary of Jesuit spirituality. This is Michael the man, the Jesuit, the priest.

Karl Rahner also wrote that "old age is a great grace, a gift, *and also* a mission—not given to everyone." Rahner praised the Jesuits for designating its elderly as those who "pray for the Society of Jesus." Michael not only prayed for the Society but his presence at Campion was a *living prayer*. Even in illness, he had his routine at Campion: prayer, listening to operas, jigsaw puzzles, movies, poetry readings with another Jesuit, and copy editing for foreign Jesuits and many others. He is a model of how to live, then to live with illness, and then to die into the risen Christ. I marveled at the edifying, patient, and non-complaining way he bore his cruel illnesses.

Michael, you did it. Congratulations! We'll miss you. You were an inspiration to us all: dedicated, urbane, erudite, gracious, witty, learned, and silently holy. We'll meet with you in the Eucharist for you are certainly in Christ. And to quote another great Jesuit who died several years ago: "It's a great old Soc.," and Jesuits like you, Michael, make it so. All this is the reason good Pope John XXIII could say: "every day is a good day to be born; every day is a good day to die."

www.ingramcontent.com/pod-product-compliance
Lightning Source LLC
Chambersburg PA
CBHW060602230426
43670CB00011B/1932